DECORATIVE WOODCARVING

DECORATIVE WOODCARVING

JEREMY WILLIAMS

GUILD OF MASTER CRAFTSMAN PUBLICATIONS LTD

First published 1994 by
Guild of Master Craftsman Publications Ltd,
116 High Street, Lewes
East Sussex BN7 1XU

© Jeremy Williams 1994

ISBN 0 946819 47 5

Photos on pages 7 and 9 are reproduced courtesy of the Board of
Trustees of the Victoria and Albert Museum.
Photo on page 129 courtesy of Binks-Bullows Ltd.
All other photographs unless otherwise credited by
David Scholes, Cober Valley Studios
Line illustrations by Tim Benké, Top Draw

Designed by Ian Hunt Design

Typeset by Central Southern Typesetters, Eastbourne

Printed and bound in Great Britain by
Hillman Printers (Frome) Ltd

This book is dedicated to those wonderful things called trees.

Through the skill of our craftsmanship and the beauty of our work may the Spirit of the Tree live on.

ACKNOWLEDGEMENTS

My thanks are due to a number of companies who assisted me during the course of writing this book, including:

Ashley Iles (Edge Tools) Ltd for permission to reproduce their photographs
Henry Taylor (Tools) Ltd for permission to reproduce their carving tool chart and for supplying samples for photography
Craft Supplies Ltd for permission to reproduce their chart of Swiss carving tools
Hegner UK Ltd and Tyme Machines plc for the photographs of their honing systems
Liberon Waxes Ltd for permission to reproduce text from their catalogue and for kindly verifying my data on wood dyes.

I am indebted to William Sampson, the editor of *Fine Woodworking* magazine, and American carver Fred Cogelow for providing details of American woods. Likewise, I thank Tom Darby of Wamberal, New South Wales for the information on Australian carving woods.

Carvers Valerie Hadley, Fred Cogelow, Peter Boex, Ray Gonzalez and Rod Naylor, and past students of mine Joy Ferguson and Doug Mason, kindly gave permission to reproduce photographs of their work.

Thanks to art historian Rozanne Arnold for checking historical facts, to William Chapman for dealing with aspects of technical drawing, and to Ian Cox and Alan Pearce of Rozen Furniture.

I am grateful to photographer David Scholes of Cober Valley Studios, Helston, for all his time and patience; to my editor, at GMC Publications, Liz Inman, for her guidance; and to Cherry Ekins, who pulled all the material together.

To my wife, Jeane, my special thanks for her unstinting support.

Finally, my thanks to all the other individuals and companies who assisted me in producing this book.

CONTENTS

INTRODUCTION

Go into the old churches and stately homes of England, or the cathedrals of France, Spain or Germany, and you will find many fine examples of decorative carving. Or perhaps look at the beautiful work produced by craftsmen in India, China or Japan; by the Maori carvers of New Zealand; or the work from Bali and Polynesia. Even in today's busy world there are still many quiet corners where men and women use the traditional methods of relief carving to express their artistic ideas.

Unfortunately, though, many carvers, and particularly beginners, tend to overlook the techniques which can be generalized as decorative woodcarving, and in doing so deny themselves much scope for expressing their ideas. Wood is not as malleable as clay, and doesn't have the inherent strength of bronze, so it is sometimes impossible to produce an idea in a three-dimensional form satisfactorily by carving in the round. But by working in relief virtually all designs are possible. The techniques described in this book are traditional, and can be used for a wide array of ornamental and functional purposes: panels and wall-plaques, screens, furniture decoration, and even everyday items like breadboards.

Many books have been written about wood sculpture, but in recent years there seem to have been few devoted solely to decorative forms of carving. This seems to me a very great pity, for there is no doubt that by learning the techniques commonly used by carvers in days gone by, one's carving skill can be greatly improved. There is also the added bonus that these techniques can be useful when texture treatments have to be applied to three-dimensional work.

Decorative carving is an extensive subject, and many volumes could be filled with practical examples, but when the basic techniques are examined and analysed they divide into clear and simple categories: low relief, high relief, incised, intaglio, and pierced carving. And one of the virtues is that none of the various techniques is difficult to learn.

LOW RELIEF is undoubtedly the most popular style, and is widely used in furniture carving. Basically it consists of removing a minimal amount of background wood – usually not more than ¼in (6mm) at most – to create the contours of the chosen pattern.

HIGH RELIEF carving, as the term implies, requires the removal of a greater depth of background – usually around 1–2in (25–50mm), but at times the working depth needed may be more. In extreme cases a high relief carving can assume virtually three-dimensional proportions, and be built up with blocks glued to the background wood.

INCISED carving in its simplest form is literally drawing a design with a cutting tool on the surface of the wood. This technique is useful when a totally flat surface must be retained, such as a chair seat or back, or for a simple picture. However, incised carving can be more effective if some contour modelling is carried out in the actual design – a treatment known as modified incised carving. Another method of decorating a flat surface is to use chip carving techniques, which employ geometric designs made with angular incised cuts.

INTAGLIO work involves producing a negative image, and is mainly used for creating designs on items such as butter moulds. The treatment can also be effective for areas of detail, such as small leaves, incorporated in a relief carving.

PIERCED carving is the technique employed when wood not forming part of the actual design is removed by a series of cut-outs. It is similar to fretwork, and can be used for screens or wall plaques.

Over the many years I have instructed beginners, my approach has been to introduce the basic guide-lines of technique, and then encourage the student to interpret his or her own design. Why be obliged to carve an oak leaf, just because I say so, when you really want to carve a rose? In this book I have adopted the same method.

There are practical instructions for each technique, but it is up to you, the reader, to formulate your own design or reproduce the example used, as you choose. Whichever course you take, I very much hope you will enjoy the experience. This is not intended to be a book of designs and patterns, but rather the means to help you embark on a voyage of adventure into decorative carving. My objective is to allow the reader (be you an accomplished craftsman in other forms of woodwork, or a complete beginner) to learn something of lasting value about this art form.

For the benefit of readers new to carving, this book not only covers the actual techniques, but also ranges over the selection of suitable woods, and the choice of tools and their care. These are fundamental to success. Both styling and technical drawing are covered, as well as suitable finishing treatments, including the use of colour.

In Chapter 14 you will find advice on safety. Carving is not a dangerous activity, but it obviously pays to take care when you are using sharp tools and mechanical cutting instruments. Please read this chapter carefully before you attempt any carving.

Finally, a note on how the dimensions used in this book are described. Since it is not written for any specific group, there will clearly be some readers who prefer to work in inches and others who use metric measurements. I have chosen to indicate both, but for obvious purposes I have on occasion opted to use the nearest practical metric equivalent rather than a true conversion.

JEREMY WILLIAMS
Traboe, Helston, Cornwall, 1993

CHAPTER ONE

HISTORICAL ASPECTS

The decision to take up woodcarving is usually combined with a great enthusiasm to seize a piece of wood and just get going. This is fine if you simply want to whittle away, but for anything more adventurous you will undoubtedly find it useful to look at the history of carving and the types of work done through the ages. Even a brief study will help you to answer vital questions such as 'What shall I carve?' and 'In what style shall I carve it?' and give you an understanding of why certain tools or species of wood are more suitable for one style of work rather than another. It is also inspiring, as you admire a beautiful old carving, to think that it was created by somebody who was also once a complete beginner!

Nobody knows precisely when wood was first carved, but it is reasonable to assume that it was practised by primitive man – if only to notch his club every time he battered a sabre-toothed tiger. As wood is a perishable material, however, any examples of prehistoric carving have long since vanished. You can still see examples of Egyptian tomb carvings dating back more than 4,000 years, but these are not really decorative woodcarvings in the modern sense of the phrase.

The real history of decorative carving starts in the medieval era, with the Saxons and Normans. Quality of workmanship has always been governed by the availability of suitable tools, and it is interesting to note that carvings from the 10th and 11th centuries differ very much in execution from those of later periods, purely because early work was carried out by carpenters using only simple chisels.

By the 13th and 14th centuries purpose-made carving tools had been developed, and with them an increasing mastery of carving techniques. At this point carving styles began to diversify as craftsmen became influenced by different architectural styles, but two main themes emerged: the Gothic and the classical. The popularity of these two schools has waxed and waned down the centuries, following the dictates of fashion, and at times they have even been intermingled, with somewhat dubious results.

The Gothic style can be traced to north European influences, which were spread far and wide by the warlike races of the region. For centuries past, Vikings, Danes and other marauders had rampaged around with considerable enthusiasm, carrying with them the aesthetic ideals of their culture. For example, in 911 AD one Ruric the Jute led an excursion into Russia and founded a dynasty that reigned for some 600 years, taking with him northern ideas of decoration to combine with the eastern styles of the conquered territory.

While early Gothic carving, such as may be seen in many late Norman churches, was executed in a somewhat heavy manner, this school developed to produce open tracery work of fine quality. By the time of the early Tudors in the late 15th century, the Perpendicular Gothic style was extensively used in

 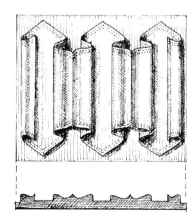

Fig 1.1 In the fifteenth century linen-fold carving was very popular as an embellishment for panelling and furniture.

Fig 1.2 This angel, carved in limewood by Tilman
Riemenschneider, is now in the Victoria and Albert Museum.

Fig 1.3 The acanthus leaf is still a familiar emblem in
woodcarving.

architectural carving. Craftsmen used woods which were readily available locally, such as oak, ash and elm.

Another milestone of the 15th century was the interest in trying to reproduce the look of fabric in wood. This led to the development of the well-known linenfold pattern (Fig 1.1), which was extensively used for both architectural panelling and for decorative embellishment on furniture.

One of the greatest exponents of the Gothic style of carving (indeed, one of the two greatest carvers ever known) was Tilman Riemenschneider. Born in southern Germany in 1460, Riemenschneider devoted most of his adult life to the creation of extraordinarily detailed religious carvings (Fig 1.2). Up until his death in 1531 he worked consistently in the area lying between Salzburg, Munich and Frankfurt, where many of his carvings can still be seen in churches.

Meanwhile, in the eastern Mediterranean, the classical style of carving was becoming standard. Derived from the classical art of early Roman times, it acquired strong classical Greek and even Persian influences after the Roman emperor Constantine transferred his seat of government to Byzantium (now Istanbul) in 324 AD. The Greek acanthus leaf emblem (Fig 1.3) became the bedrock of decorative carving in this region for the next thousand years, used either on its own or linked with Christian symbols.

By the middle of the 16th century carvers in western Europe were beginning to turn their backs on the schematic thought of medieval Gothic styles and were looking to the classical style for inspiration. The new influence began in Italy and rapidly spread to neighbouring countries, gaining a particularly strong foothold in the Low Countries. The transition did not happen overnight, though, and for some time the pendulum swung to and fro between the Italian/Flemish classical style and Gothic patterns. Spain played an important role in the spread of the new ideas. She was a dominant force in European politics during this period, and many Flemish craftsmen went to work on Spanish churches and cathedrals.

In England, classically inspired styles really became popular following the restoration of the monarchy in 1660. Charles II brought European ideas with him from his exile in France; his successor, William III (William and Mary) imported Dutch tastes from his home in the Netherlands. After the strictures of the Puritans, a new decorative style was received with considerable relief and pleasure, and Italian curvilinear designs were much in demand. Cabinetmakers emerged as craftsmen in their own right, whereas previously most furniture had been made by joiners.

The 17th-century expansion of commercial frontiers was also important, not least because woods other than common native species became more readily available. Although oak continued to be

**Fig 1.4 An extravagantly carved chair, typical of the
Chippendale style.**

favoured for architectural work, lime wood and pear wood were increasingly used for decorative carving in the latter part of the century. By the early 1700s walnut had become popular, imported from both mainland Europe and North America. Mahogany was also beginning to be used.

The period from around 1730 to the early 1800s is truly described as the golden age of woodcarving. Carvers were elevated beyond the ranks of joiners, and even cabinetmakers. They were able to dictate how things should be carved, rather than working to prescribed designs. Gilding was held in high regard, so carvers either worked closely with gilders or did the gilding themselves. The rich and noble spent money on decorative carving at a phenomenal rate, as much to indicate their status as for any appreciation of the craftsmanship involved.

English carving of this period was much enriched by the work of Grinling Gibbons who, jointly with Riemenschneider, can lay claim to the title of 'the world's best carver'. Born in Rotterdam in 1648 of English parents, Gibbons moved to England at the age of 20 and worked there until his death in 1741. He established a unique style of carving which, while classical in foundation, eschewed the symmetrical and well-tested proportions of the true Classical style in favour of exuberant asymmetry. High-relief swags embellished with swirls and curls are typical of the work. He used flowers of every type with total abandon and even carved nutmegs and other fruits. Cherubs bound forth through clusters of fruits and birds peck at seed heads with natural grace.

This flamboyancy burst upon conservative architects and patrons like a thunderclap, shaking them from their resistance to change. Gibbons was an avid collector of paintings, so contemporary artists may well have inspired him, but he was undoubtedly indebted to the architect Sir Christopher Wren (1632–1723) for his rise to prominence, and other support came from the contemporary diarist Sir John Evelyn. With friends of such eminence, Gibbons soon gained royal patronage.

Much of Gibbons' work was carried out in the opulent, dramatic and exciting baroque style, but he was also capable of more restrained carving. His prodigious output led to the belief that he employed many carvers rather than undertaking all the work himself, and this theory was recently reinforced when restoration work was carried out after the fire at Hampton Court Palace. On taking down some fire-damaged carvings, it was discovered that some of the pieces had originally been fitted together upside down – surely the work of an apprentice rather than a master craftsman.

The rococo period which followed the baroque was more restrained in style, with spirals and diagonal elements depicted less strongly. It was particularly popular in France, but Thomas Johnson, who died around 1778, was a well-known carver of English rococo work.

During this golden age of carving the art of cabinetmaking also came to the fore. Men like Thomas Chippendale (1718–1789) and his son, also Thomas (1749–1822), used decorative carving extravagantly on their furniture (Fig 1.4). Hepplewhite, who died in 1786, was also fond of carving on furniture, but used it in a more restrained manner (Fig 1.5). Duncan Phyfe (1768–1854) is regarded by many as the greatest of all American cabinetmakers. Much of his work is decorated with carved leaves, lions' feet, dogs' feet, Prince of Wales feathers, wheatears, and other embellishments.

But carvers were by no means limited to architectural work and furniture decoration. During the Georgian period one's means of transportation became a way of keeping up with fashion, so carriages, cabs and sedan chairs were all emblazoned with every known device and intricate carving – the Coronation Coach is a familiar example of this kind of extravaganza.

During Queen Victoria's reign, from the middle to the end of the 19th century, the Industrial Revolution led to the introduction of more advanced production methods. Machines were invented to handle much of the hard and repetitive work. A carving machine patented in England in 1845 is thought to have been developed to cope with the enormous volume of repetitive carving entailed in the restoration of the Houses of Parliament; another was patented in America in 1848.

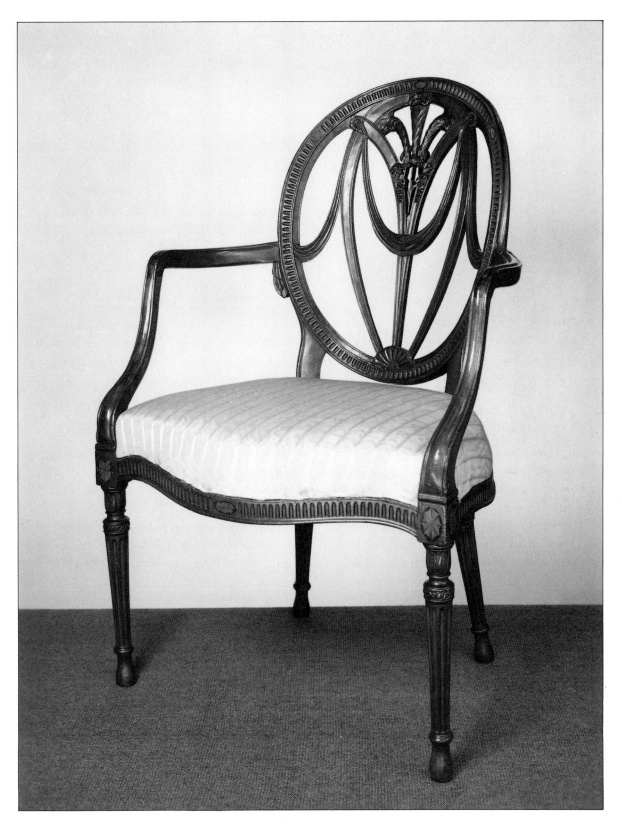

Fig 1.5 The carving of Hepplewhite furniture was more restrained.

Fig 1.6 An example of late-Victorian mock-Gothic, carved
on a piece of furniture.

Victorian carving primarily followed the nostalgic fashion of copying 'antique' styles redolent of the 'glorious past', and much of this imitation was not carried out with spectacular expertise. There was a Gothic revival (correctly known as 'Gothick' to distinguish it from the real thing), and a fondness for over-embellishment which does not always appeal to modern tastes (Fig 1.6). The Victorian love of dead game birds and other victims of the chase may seem equally unappealing, but nevertheless useful ideas for subjects can be found by studying 19th-century carvings. At the other end of the scale, William Morris (1834–1896) did much to initiate a handcraft revival through the Arts and Crafts movement during this period. One of the effects was to restore respect for furniture of simple design.

After the First World War fashion swung away from decorative carving; and its intensive labour element had in any case become too costly. More functional styles evolved in the mid-1920s, followed by the 'utility' furniture of the 1940s and 1950s. The Scandinavian furniture popular in the 1960s was equally unsuited to decorative carving, so for much of the 20th century the craft has seen bleak years of decline.

But to some degree the wheel of fortune is turning once more. Decorative carving is creeping back, little by little, and is beginning to be seen on furniture in modest amounts. The future looks brighter now than for many years. And in the meanwhile, we are fortunate in having a wealth of carving history to study in our churches, public buildings, museums, stately homes, and even antiques shops. Looking at the work of past craftsmen, both well known and anonymous, stimulates ideas and extends the horizons of carvers today.

CHAPTER TWO

CHOOSING THE RIGHT WOOD

While in theory it is possible to carve all and every species of wood, clearly some are more suitable than others. Knowing something about the structure of timber, and about how trees grow, will pay dividends when you actually start carving. Also, it is important to know how to choose the right wood for the work you plan to do, and how to store it so it stays in prime condition.

In the timber trade the broad-leafed types are categorized as hardwoods and those with needle-shaped leaves as softwoods. But it is important to remember these are only general descriptions – they may have little bearing on whether the wood is either hard or soft. For example lime, or its American cousin basswood, is one of the easiest woods to carve, yet because it is a broad-leafed tree it comes into the hardwood listing. Yew, on the other hand, being a needle-leaved evergreen is categorized as a softwood, although it is a hard wood indeed to work with cutting tools.

Many timber suppliers include details of the wood's density in their catalogues, usually shown as a figure of specific gravity or an indication of weight per cubic foot or metre. For precise identification, the Latin botanical name of the wood is also included. Lime and oak, for example, would be listed:

Lime *(Tilia spp)*, 34lb/ft^3, 540kg/m^3, SG 0.54
Oak *(Quercus spp)*, 45lb/ft^3, 720kg/m^3, SG 0.67

This clearly shows that lime is less dense than oak.

But while it can be useful to know the density figures if, say, you want to carve a rare wood for the first time, it is simpler to select a wood if you know its carving quality – easy to work, moderately hard, or hard – and whether or not it is capable of accepting fine detail (*see* the list on pages 21–22).

Timber can be broadly divided into three main groups, relating to where and how the trees originally grew. The warmer and moister the climate, the more quickly a tree will grow, which affects the type of wood to be obtained from it.

TEMPERATE CLIMATE Trees from temperate climate zones, such as Europe and parts of North America, can be either broad-leafed deciduous varieties, which drop their leaves in winter, or members of the conifer family, with needle-shaped leaves, which commonly are evergreen. Most of the popular carving woods are broad-leafed species.

EQUATORIAL CLIMATE Tropical trees are those which come from all the equatorial zones of the world. Generally they are known as tropical hardwoods. They range from varieties producing rare and exotic woods, such as rosewood, through to the more well-known mahogany types. While widely used in the past, many are now listed as endangered species; although some timber suppliers conform to a policy of only buying from areas of reafforestation.

COLD CLIMATE There are the trees which come either from the colder zones of the world, such as Scandinavia, Baltic countries and Canada, or which grow in a temperate climate but at a high altitude. While they may not be used extensively for carving in Britain, in their home countries they are popular. Generally they fall into the softwood classification.

HOW WOOD IS FORMED

In simple terms all trees, irrespective of where they grow, have similar component parts (Fig 2.1). There is an outer protective casing, the bark; a growing area, sapwood; and an inert stable section for upright

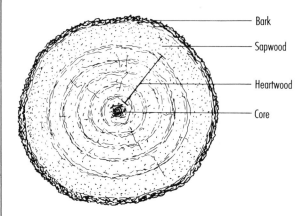

Fig 2.1 **Horizontal cross-section of tree trunk showing main component parts.**

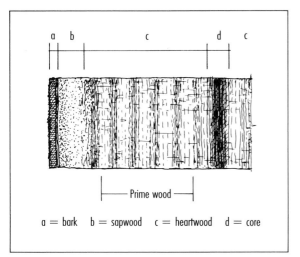

Fig 2.2 Vertical cross-section of tree trunk showing prime heartwood area.

While most cells run vertically through the trunk, they also follow the way the branches grow. Some trees have pronounced storage cells which lie more horizontally. These are medullary rays, which can be decorative in furniture, but are more a source of trouble to the carver than an advantage. Their density is quite different from the surrounding wood, and they are invariably lines of weakness.

ANNUAL RINGS

Every year throughout its life a tree grows, increasing not only in height but also in the girth of its trunk. The amount of growth is dependent upon external factors, such as the amount of rainfall, ambient temperature, and number of hours of sunlight. This cycle of growth can be seen as annual rings when a tree is felled.

There are two periods in the year when trees living in temperate climates actually grow, and the pronounced climatic variations between winter and summer affects the growth cycle. Most new wood is formed in spring and early summer – spring growth – but later in the year secondary growth takes place, forming late wood. The annual rings reflect this growth pattern: spring growth is represented by wider bands, as this is when the bulk of new wood is formed, while narrower bands show late growth (Fig 2.3).

strength, heartwood. Many trees also have a central core of pith.

Of these the only part which is of any real value for carving is the heartwood. The prime part lies 2in (50mm) in from both the sapwood and the central core (Fig 2.2).

All wood is made up of cells, used by trees for holding nutriment in solution and for water storage. Generally they are similar to bundles of drinking straws. It is important for the carver to know how well the cells are bonded together, since this affects the quality of work that can be produced (*see* page 20).

Fig 2.3 Horizontal cross-section of tree trunk showing vertical cell structure, medullary rays, and differing annual rings representing spring growth and late wood.

You should note that late growth bands are darker, because the wood contains more resin and is harder than spring growth. The difference is most marked in conifers, and the resulting variations in wood density can make carving difficult. Similarly, broad-leafed trees, which grow very quickly, will show a distinct variation in ring pattern, with soft spring growth and harder bands of late wood. Slow-growing trees generally have more uniform, more narrowly spaced rings, producing timber of a more even density with which you will achieve better results.

The growth pattern of tropical trees is generally more even than that of trees from temperate zones, as the sun is more consistently overhead and there are fewer seasonal variations of climate. However, habitat has a profound influence on the tree's growth: a tree growing halfway up a mountain in the tropics will experience totally different climatic conditions to a tree at sea level, and will grow accordingly.

This is also true of trees anywhere in the world. For example, an oak down in the far south-west of England will grow more quickly and produce a lower quality grade of timber than one in, say, Scotland. This is why cold climate trees need to be differentiated from their temperate-zone cousins. A Scots pine on home ground is one thing, as the cold climate will cause slow growth and produce

Fig 2.4 The normal through and through planking process.

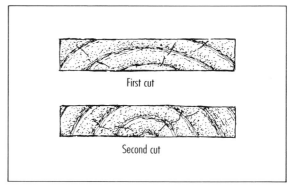

Fig 2.5 Horizontal cross-section of first and second cuts in through and through planking, showing annual rings arcing across planks.

good carving timber; as an alien in a temperate climate it is quite another matter, and may not be suitable for carving at all. Your timber merchant will be able to help you choose woods from the right climatic source.

TIMBER CONVERSION

Of the various ways that trees are cut into usable timber, the most common method is to saw the trunk through and through into boards (Fig 2.4). These can be of any pre-determined thickness, but will usually range from around 1in (25mm) to 4in (100mm). Most relief carving, except very high relief, is carried out using planks, or boards, between 1in (25mm) and 2in (50mm) thick.

Fig 2.5 shows the effect through and through planking has on the annual ring configuration. Note that the peripheral planks have the annual rings arcing through their width. But planks from the middle part of the tree's girth have the rings placed nearer to the vertical as shown in Fig 2.6. This type of wood is described as quarter sawn.

Fig 2.6 Horizontal cross-section through quarter sawn midway cut.

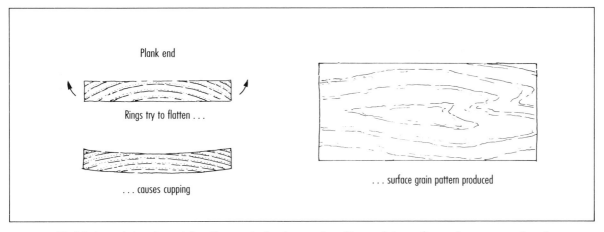

Fig 2.7 Annual rings in peripherally-cut planks, the cupping effect, and the surface grain pattern produced.

Fig 2.8 Annual rings in quarter sawn (midway cut) planks, and the surface grain pattern produced.

When the rings lie near to the horizontal (peripherally-cut planks), they produce circular or flowing grain patterns. But when the rings are closer to the vertical (quarter sawn or midway cut), the grain will be more linear. Figs 2.7 and 2.8 show how the angle of the annual rings affects the grain seen on the top and bottom surfaces.

Note the upward pointing arrows in Fig 2.7. These indicate how the wood may distort or cup as the annual rings tend to straighten from an arc to the horizontal. The quarter-sawn wood shown in Fig 2.8 is more stable, but remember that the straighter lines may cause the grain to appear too obtrusive.

To prevent cupping spoiling the look of a carving it is usual to work with the annual rings pointing upwards, as shown in Fig 2.9. If there is any

Fig 2.9 Prevent cupping by working with the annual rings pointing upwards.

distortion only the face of the piece will become bowed, which shows less. A plaque hanging on a wall, for example, could tolerate some bowing without its being noticed. Both cupping and bowing

Fig 2.10 Cupping and bowing are minimized by cutting a plank lengthways.

are minimized when the board is cut longways down the middle (Fig 2.10).

When carving inset panels for furniture, or any item which must retain a flat base, such as a breadboard, use quarter sawn timber for the sake of stability. Any visual dominance of the grain lines can usually be reduced by selecting a wood with a bland grain, such as sycamore.

SELECTING AND BUYING WOOD

Buying suitable carving wood, whether home-grown or imported, is fairly straightforward. The best starting point is to look through any of the popular woodworking magazines. They all carry advertisements for stockists. A good supplier will be able to offer boards of a wide range of woods, and in a variety of sizes. He will be able to tell you how dry the wood is and how it was seasoned. Later you may wish to buy from a timber yard which keeps stocks of freshly cut wood. You will be able to buy it more cheaply, but you will have to wait a couple of years or more for the wood to season.

Unfortunately, these days not all the wood on offer is of prime quality, and you do need to be selective. Avoid any wood with obvious faults – splits, knots or decay. Trees can have internal splits, shakes, caused by storm damage or poor felling (Fig 2.11).

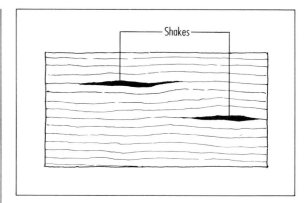

Fig 2.11 Avoid timber with shakes.

These only come to light when the wood is planked. Similar, but more difficult to spot, are shakes which form radially. You may see them as diagonal lines in the board. Sometimes if you bend the wood across its width they will be visible.

Areas which are pithy will never produce good results. Pithy areas contain soft tissue, and are easy to detect either by sight or trial cutting. They can be caused by over-rapid growth, or by rot. The most common type of rot is due to fungus, and is generally known as dote (Fig 2.12). Fungus stain can penetrate deeply into the wood – look for blotches of darker colour on lime and sycamore, as both these woods are prone to the effects of damp. Similarly, elm suffers from fungus attack if poorly ventilated – look for white powder on the surface. Bad storage can also cause wood surfaces to look stained.

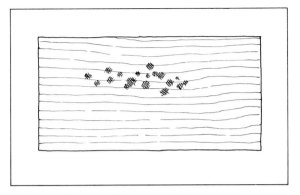

Fig 2.12 Telltale spots of dote fungus.

Most beginners try to be far too economical. Be prepared for some wastage. For example, you frequently find board ends have started to split. They might not seem to be very bad, and you could be tempted to ignore them – but don't! Even a tiny split no thicker than a hair's width can quickly open up. Never work right up to the original ends: cut back by 2in (50mm) or more and look again (Fig 2.13).

If there is a knot, avoid it. Only seldom will it not detract from or spoil the overall look of your work. Knots shrink, split or even fall out, and the density of the surrounding wood will be different from the rest of the timber.

SEASONING

Before it can be used, timber must be seasoned to reduce its moisture content and lessen the naturally occurring tension present in all growing trees. Seasoning can take place in two main ways, air drying and kiln-drying, or a combination of the two.

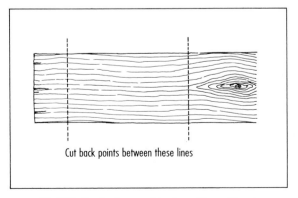

Cut back points between these lines

Fig 2.13 Cut back to avoid edge splits and knots.

In the air-drying method, cut planks are stacked with spacer sticks in between them. Known as being 'in stick', the wood is kept in the open and left to dry down to the ambient humidity (Fig 2.14). This takes roughly a year for each inch (25mm) of plank thickness. The slow maturing of the wood means that most, if not all, natural tension is also eliminated.

Generally, air-dried timber carves best, but you should remember that it will only be as dry as the outside humidity. This is always greater than

Fig 2.14 Air-drying timber in stick.

humidity levels in houses, especially those with central heating. Before you use any air-dried wood, it is a wise precaution to store it for three months or more in a well-ventilated workshop or shed. If you take fresh wood straight into the dry atmosphere of most modern homes you will be courting trouble.

The old saying, grandfather cut down the tree and sawed it into planks, father seasoned it, and his son used it, is certainly very true.

A quicker method for extracting moisture is kiln-drying, which relies on controlled dehumidification to produce low levels of retained moisture with little subsequent shrinkage. But the drying processes result in the wood being more brittle, tougher and sometimes accompanied by a slight colour change. Not all the natural tension will be released.

Much timber, though, undergoes a combination of the two processes. After air-drying it is reduced to a lower level of moisture content by a short stretch in a kiln. This timber will carve reasonably, but perhaps not quite as well as when just air-dried. However, since there is less risk of shrinkage later on it can prove suitable for furniture work.

STORAGE

Store your timber stock in a dry and airy covered place away from direct sunlight. Inside the workshop may be too warm, especially in winter with heating running. Lay the timber on spacer sticks, which should be about 18in (450mm) apart for long planks. The sticks should be around ½in (10mm) square and preferably cut from the same wood, or staining may occur.

As a precaution against splitting many carvers seal the ends of the boards using either wax or flat oil-based paint. This prevents any remaining moisture drying out too quickly while the wood is stored.

You can get meters to measure the moisture content of wood, but in practice this is not really necessary, especially if you buy supplies from a reliable source. When in doubt the wood can be weighed at regular intervals to check if it is drying out. But generally if you buy sensibly and keep the wood for a reasonable period of time you shouldn't have any problems. You may have to start with kiln-dried stock until your air-dried wood has had time to stabilize.

FIGURING AND COLOUR

Broadly, the surface figuring you see is made up of annual rings seen lengthwise. But it also has small flecks, which are cells lying at an angle in the wood, and perhaps some medullary rays. All of these will have a visual effect when carved, and need to be taken into account.

Woods vary in colour. The same type of tree grown in differing soil conditions will produce wood of a different shade, due to the effect of minerals and salts in the soil.

GRAIN

When you look at a piece of wood you don't know which way up it grew, but if you run your hand over the surface you will find one direction is smoother than the other. This shows the lie of the grain (Fig 2.15). Cuts with the lie of the grain will be shiny, while cuts in the opposite direction will be rough. Wherever possible you should carve with the broad lie of the grain.

Trees which grew straight and tall produce straight grain timber; those which developed in any direction they pleased usually produce twisted grain (Fig 2.16 (*a*) and (*b*)). Twisted grain is more difficult to carve, since the direction of cutting has to vary, and the grain effect may not be advantageous. Avoid it if possible.

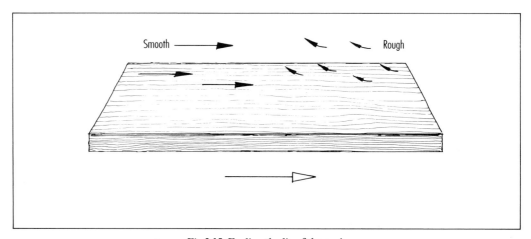

Fig 2.15 Feeling the lie of the grain.

Some trees spiral as they grow, and when their wood is planked the grain is not uniform in the way it lies. This interlocked grain is frequently found in tropical trees. It is always a problem, since it is difficult to cut cleanly. You can recognize interlocked grain because some grain flecks run the length of the wood, while others lie in bands at an angle (Fig 2.17).

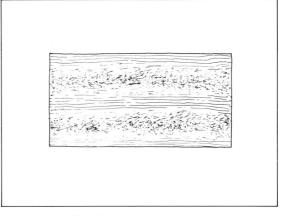

Fig 2.17 Interlocked grain.

FITTING THE WOOD TO THE CARVING

To a great extent the success of a carving can be marred by simply using the wrong wood. Even the most experienced carver would be hard put to produce fine and delicate detail if the timber is just not capable of accepting it; or the subtle lines of a design can be negated by too much colour in the

wood. So choosing the right timber for the carving you intend to do is very important, and depends on a combination of scale, detail, and colour and figuring.

S C A L E is important, because small or delicate carvings require a wood in which the grain will not dominate the design. Strong grain lines, or marked figuring in the wood, are better suited to large or robust work.

D E T A I L of carving is also a consideration – intricate designs necessitate using a close-grained timber. These are generally the types listed as easy or moderately easy to work.

C O L O U R A N D F I G U R I N G play a part. Wherever possible it is best to avoid wood which has a pronounced colour variation, as this can detract from the visual effect of the design. Equally, heavily figured wood can present problems if the figuring runs contrary to the direction of the main elements in the carving.

CELL STRUCTURE

It is also important to know how well the cells in the wood bond to each other, not only individually but also in making up the total growth pattern of the timber. Some woods, like lime, cherry and sycamore, are very stable; their structure is compact, with tiny cells each well bonded to its neighbours. The

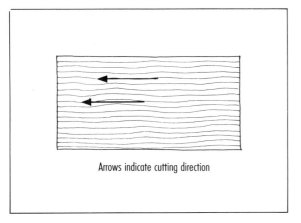

Arrows indicate cutting direction

Fig 2.16 (a) Straight grain.

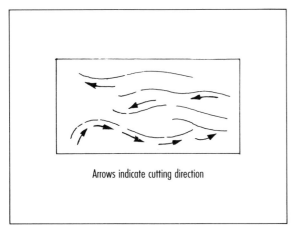

Arrows indicate cutting direction

Fig 2.16 (b) Twisted grain.

resultant strength and uniform texture make these woods ideal for carving fine and delicate detail.

In other woods cell size can be larger, and the inter-cell bonding may be weak. While this may not affect the strength of the timber for normal joinery, such weakness will become apparent in delicate carving. Oak is a typical example: well known for its inherent strength, it has relatively large cells and weak inter-cell bonding. It is consequently difficult to carve oak with fine detail, unless the carver is skilled, as pieces will invariably snap off. Test the strength of cell bonding by trying to break off a small piece from a plank corner with your thumbnail (*see* Fig 2.18). If the wood breaks easily, it has weak inter-cell bonding.

Woods with an interlocked grain can have a sandwich-like appearance in the cell configuration. In some areas the cells will be set longitudinally, while in others they lie tangentially to the length of the timber. Bonding will be weak wherever these areas meet. You will often see this in tropical timbers, making them more suited to robust styles of carving.

You will find it helpful to know a couple of technical terms used frequently when describing practical aspects of a carving. End-grain means any cut surface which exposes the ends of the timber's

Fig 2.19 End-grain, and cross-grain or short-grain carving.

cells. Think of the end of a plank. Short-grain or cross-grain refers to elements of a design carved at an angle to the run of the grain – they fall across the path of the grain and the figure pattern on the wood. Fig 2.19 illustrates these terms.

SUITABLE CARVING WOODS

When considering woods best suited for carving, we are principally interested in slow-growing trees giving wood of an even density, and especially those which produce good diameter trunks. This will allow planks of a reasonable width (above 6in; 150mm) to be obtained.

Remember, too, that woods with a delicate grain are ideal for working intricate designs, as an obtrusive grain would be totally undesirable. But when the design is fairly bold, woods with a more definite grain pattern can be used. Generally their density will also be greater, and, while somewhat harder to work than woods with a delicate grain, they will produce a more durable polished surface.

L I M E (*Tilia vulgaris/cordata*) Easy to work. Undoubtedly the most suitable wood to start with, lime is known as the carver's wood and is ideal for detailed decoration. The cell structure is very small, and each cell is so well bonded to its neighbour that the chances of the wood fracturing when carved thinly are minimized. It can be straw-coloured, or even lighter. The grain is seldom distinctive.

Fig 2.18 Test cell strength by breaking off a small corner of the plank.

SYCAMORE (*Acer pseudoplatanus*) Varies from easy to moderately difficult to work, depending on the drying method and the length of time it has been seasoned. Slightly harder than lime, but with the same characteristics of small cells so it takes detail well. It is very light in colour, near-white in the best grades, but can contain streaks of silver-grey. Grain is subtle, frequently with a ripple pattern.

CHESTNUT Sweet/Spanish (*Castenea sativa*) Moderately easy to work. In many respects chestnut resembles flat sawn oak, but without the medullary rays. Pale brown in colour. The grain is normally straight, but coarse in texture.

ELM (*Ulmus spp*) Difficult to work. This distinctive wood is becoming difficult to obtain in good quality due to the ravages of Dutch elm disease. Of the many types, English elm (*Ulmus procera*) is light to dark brown in colour, while wych elm (*Ulmus glabra*, also known as northern elm) has an attractive green streak to the brown grain.

CHERRY (*Prunus avium*) Moderately easy to work. This is a most attractive wood which takes detail well. Colour is pinkish-brown, sometimes with a green streak. Grain is usually straight.

PEAR (*Pyrus communis*) Difficult to work. Close-grained and quite hard, pear can be ideal for small inset panels in furniture. The wood is strong and tough, but does have a tendency to distort and split. Natural colour is bland, although it takes stain well, but pearwood which has been steamed as part of the seasoning process is pleasingly pink. Even grain and fine texture with little figuring.

WALNUT (*Juglans regia*) Moderately difficult to work. A delightful wood to carve; well worth its expense. Use with discretion as its figured grain can be sympathetic to, or detract from, the design. British walnut is dark brown with much figuring; walnut from France, widely available in the UK, is generally lighter in colour with a straighter grain. Both are the same species and take fine detail well.

OAK (*Quercus spp*) Difficult to work. Extensively used for ecclesiastical and architectural carving, and still employed today, oak is not a wood to consider until you have built up some expertise, as it is fairly tough and prone to split. Colour is light brown, darkening with age; brown oak shows the timber has been attacked by beefsteak fungus, which causes a chemical colour change to take place. Texture is coarse with large rays.

MAHOGANY (*Swietenia spp*) Moderately difficult to work. The tropical hardwood undoubtedly most universally used in woodworking generally. There are many species and sub-species, all of which tend to have similar carving properties. It is worth mentioning two important factors. Firstly, while much exquisite carving was carried out in mahogany a hundred years or more ago, it is nowadays impossible to buy new wood of a similar quality. It just doesn't exist. Secondly, there is the moral issue of whether the timber available today is ecologically sustainable. Many woodworkers are, for this reason alone, turning away completely from the use of tropical hardwoods; others try to ensure their supplies come from renewable sources. You could try to find some reclaimed material – old and broken pieces of furniture can easily make suitable carving wood.

SCOTS PINE (*Pinus sylvestris*) Moderately difficult to work. Classified as a softwood. Also known as redwood, the better Scots pine is widely distributed throughout the colder parts of Europe, especially Scandinavia. Colour is light brown. While reasonably easy to work, the wood is prone to knots and you should expect some density variation.

YEW (*Taxus baccata*) Difficult to work. Despite its botanical classification as a softwood, this is a tough timber. It is very hard, but can be used effectively for small carvings – though you should expect a high element of wastage from knots, holes and ingrowing bark. Colour varies from light to rich brown, with purple tints which fade with exposure to daylight. Usually has a 'wild' grain.

ASH (*Fraxinus excelsior*) Moderately easy to work. Can be prone to split, making it unsuitable for fine detail. Generally pale or almost white in colour, but can have brown heartwood. Old trees of large girth can produce a mass of even figuring at right angles to the grain, which is known as olive ash or ripple ash. The ripple often has treacle-coloured streaks.

POPULAR AMERICAN CARVING WOODS

BASSWOOD (*Tilia americana*) Easy to work. Also known as American lime, basswood is similar to its European cousin and shares the same carving properties. Colour is creamy white, sometimes pale brown. Straight grain and even texture.

BUTTERNUT (*Juglans cinerea*) Moderately difficult to work. Also known as white walnut, butternut is difficult to obtain in Britain. The wood displays most of the characteristics of walnut and has similar grain patterns, but is lighter in colour. Expect some wastage.

CHERRY (*Prunus serotian*) Moderately difficult to work. The wood has good working properties, and is reddish-brown in colour. Fine grain and even texture.

RED OAK (*Quercus rubra/falcata*) Moderately difficult to work. Northern red oak *(Q. rubra)* is considered by many carvers to be superior. Colour is biscuit pink to brown. Open grain.

BLACK WALNUT (*Juglans nigra*) Difficult to work. This wood needs to be worked with care for fine detail. It is richly coloured, varying from dark brown to almost black. Grain verges on coarse, and is usually straight but sometimes wavy.

WESTERN WHITE PINE (*Pinus monticola*) Moderately easy to work. The heartwood is a pale straw colour, only slightly darker than the sapwood. It is straight grained with an even texture.

POPULAR AUSTRALIAN CARVING WOODS

HOOP PINE (*Araucaria cunninghamii*) Easy to work. The heartwood is yellow-brown to darker brown with a pinkish cast. It is straight grained with a uniform and fine texture.

HUON PINE (*Dacrydium franklinii*) Easy to work. The heartwood is a pale yellow. The sapwood is undefined. Grain is straight and of even texture.

ALPINE ASH (*Eucalyptus delegatensis*) Moderately difficult to work. The colour varies from pale to light brown with a pinkish tinge. It is straight grained with an open texture. Occasionally has interlocked or wavy grain.

BLACK BEAN (*Castanospermum australe*) Difficult to work. The heartwood is chocolate-brown figured with grey-brown streaks. It is generally straight grained though sometimes interlocked. Its texture is rather coarse.

JARRAH (*Eucalyptus marginata*) Difficult to work. The heartwood is light red to dark red and often has darker markings or speckles present. The sapwood is pale yellow to off white. Its grain is slightly interlocked and is of a coarse, even texture.

Summary
- Select only good quality wood.
- Take advice from a reputable timber supplier.
- Store your stock with care, and due regard to ventilation and temperature.
- Match the wood to the planned carving in respect of grain, colour and texture. If any of these is too dominant it can spoil the look of your work.
- Always treat your wood with respect. It may have taken 150 years to grow. You can ruin it in as many minutes.

SELECTING CARVING TOOLS

When you first look at the range of woodcarving tools available, it can seem bewildering. There are so many different shapes and sizes to choose from, so how do you start to make your selection? Happily, all differences between woodcarving tools boil down to three main distinctions.

1. The shape of the tool when viewed from head on.

2. The shape of the tool when viewed from the side.

3. The shape of the tool when viewed from above.

BLADE SHAPE – THE
HEAD-ON VIEW

Fig 3.1 represents the head-on view of woodcarving tools. It can easily be seen that all the tools are one of three basic shapes: a perfectly straight line (number 1 and 2), a curve (numbers 3 through 11 of 3.1), or a V shape (numbers 45, 39 and 41) There are a

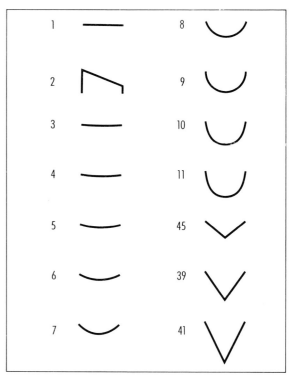

Fig 3.1 Sheffield List range of blade shapes.

THE FULL RANGE OF SWEEPS AND SIZES					1/16" 1.5	3/32" 2.25	1/8" 3	3/16" 4.5
London Pattern Straight Gouges	London Pattern Curved Gouges	London Pattern Front Bent	Spoon Bit Gouges Back Bent	Fish Tail Pattern Straight Gouges				
3	12	24	33	54 × 3	—	—	—	—
4	13	25	34	54 × 4	—	—	—	—
5	14	26	35	54 × 5	—	—	—	—
6	15	27	36	54 × 6	⌣	⌣	⌣	⌣
7	16	28	37	54 × 7	⌣	⌣	⌣	⌣
8	17	29	38	54 × 8	⌣	⌣	⌣	⌣
9	18	30	–	54 × 9	⌣	⌣	⌣	⌣
10	19	31	–	54 × 10	⌣	⌣	⌣	⌣
11	20	32	–	54 × 11	⌣	⌣	⌣	⌣

Fig 3.2 London Pattern range of blade sweeps and sizes.

few specialized tools, such as the macaroni, that have end shapes that do not fit neatly into this classification scheme. It would be rare to find a use for such a tool unless, perhaps, you were restoring antique furniture.

CHISELS AND SKEWS A tool whose head-on shape is a straight line is either a chisel (number 1) or a skew (number 2). Number 2 in Fig 3.1 actually shows the shape of the skews as they would be seen from the top. This view shows that, although the head-on view of the skew is identical to that of the chisel, that is, a straight line, it is distinguished from the chisel by having its cutting edge at an angle.

Chisels are straight-bladed tools with a bevel on both sides and are used for straight cuts. Chisels are also used to smooth carved surfaces. Skews are quite useful for the woodcarver, especially for undercutting and for cleaning out corners. If you are just starting out and need to choose one or the other, choose the skew. You will find it more versatile.

GOUGES form the largest group of woodcarving tools. Gouges are those tools whose shape, when viewed from head on, is a curve. The gouges are distinguished from each other, aside from variances in size, by the degree of curvature each displays. Numbers 3 through 9 of Fig 3.1 are true arcs of a circle. Number 9 is a half-circle. Numbers 10 and 11 have deep sides, which gives the endview of the tools a U shape. They are not true arcs of a circle.

Gouges have a bevel ground onto the bottom of the blade. When the gouge is pushed into the wood, either by hand pressure or by a blow from a mallet, the blade slices cleanly through the wood fibres and maintains a constant level of cut until pressure is let up. The bevel then forces the blade out again, leaving a smooth spoon-shaped depression. Gouges are very efficient at removing large quantities of wood. Moreover, if the tool is very sharp and the bevel is polished, the metal of the tool actually burnishes the surface of the wood as it cuts, providing you are cutting with the grain.

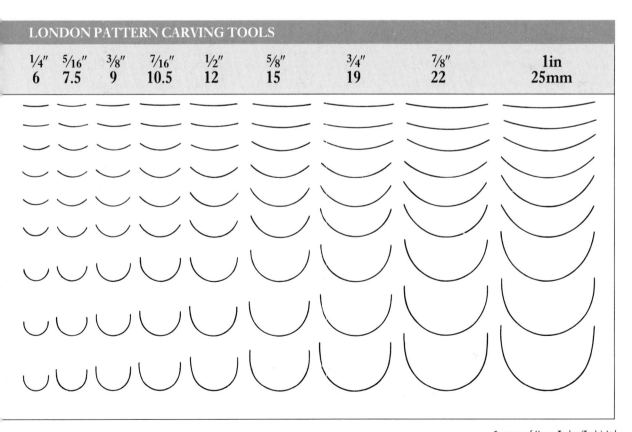

LONDON PATTERN CARVING TOOLS

¼"	⁵⁄₁₆"	³⁄₈"	⁷⁄₁₆"	½"	⅝"	¾"	⅞"	1in
6	7.5	9	10.5	12	15	19	22	25mm

Courtesy of Henry Taylor (Tools) Ltd

Fig 3.3 Three basic blades: typical English–type gouges Nos 3, 7 and 9.

VEINERS AND FLUTERS (10 and 11 of Fig 3.1) are merely gouges with U-shaped cutting edges. Their deeper sides and U shape make them useful for grooving, outlining, and hollowing out surfaces. The smaller of the U-shaped tools are called veiners, the larger, fluters, because they were traditionally used to carve the veins and flutes of acanthus foliage.

V-TOOLS OR PARTING TOOLS (39–45 of Fig 3.1), have a distinctive V shape when viewed from head on. They are normally available with the V in angles of 45°, 60° and 90°. Fig 3.13 shows a V-tool with a 60° angle. V-tools do a great deal of the carving in incised work.

SIZES OF WOODCARVING TOOLS Fig 3.2 indicates the great range of sizes woodcarving tools are offered in. The size of woodcarving tools is described by the width of the cutting edge, measured from tip to tip. Measurements are given either in imperial measurements or metric, depending on the manufacturer. Most manufacturers offer sizes ranging from $\frac{1}{16}$in (1.5mm) to 1in (25mm), but larger sizes can be found.

BLADE SHAPE –
THE SIDE VIEW

When viewed from the side, the blades of woodcarving tools can be seen to be either straight or bent (see Fig 3.5). The bent tools follow three main styles: curved (number 4), spoon-bent (numbers 5, 6, 7 and 8) and back-bent (number 12). Straight tools are the most often used tools and are used for all ordinary work. Curved tools are used for working shallow hollows. Spoon-bent tools, whose longitudinal shape has a shorter, more abrupt curve, are used for working in deeper hollows. Back-bent tools are used to work convex surfaces (see Fig 3.14).

The dog-leg chisel (number 11) is an exception to the three common bends seen in tool blades. The dog-leg chisel finds quite a bit of use, especially in cleaning up recessed areas and in deep undercutting. The bent design allows the cutting edge of the tool access to hard-to-reach areas.

BLADE SHAPE – THE TOP VIEW

When viewed from the top, the blades of gouges can be seen to vary in shape. Basic gouges have sides that are parallel from the cutting edge to where the handle normally begins. These gouges are recommended for the beginner. They readily accept a blow from the mallet. Moreover, when such a gouge is reground, the shape and size of its cutting edges is maintained. Gouges with parallel sides will last through many regrindings.

All other gouges, when viewed from above, will be seen to taper, to a greater or lesser degree, toward the tang (again *see* Fig 3.5). The fishtail, whether it be a fishtail gouge (number 13) or a fishtail chisel (number 14) exhibits a dramatic taper from the cutting edge to the tang. This taper, or wasting away of the metal, weakens the tool. However, because there is less metal behind the cutting edge, these tools can be used in areas where the straight side of a basic gouge would knock or scrape against the work, fouling it. Moreover, the taper allows for greater visibility.

Besides a loss of blade strength, the main disadvantage of tapered tools is that they lose their shape and size upon being reground.

HANDLES

The shape of the English carving tool evolved centuries ago, and was primarily determined by the hardness of the oak traditionally used for much of the work (such as you generally find in old churches, for example), and the need to carry out most of the carving using a mallet. These factors dictated a relatively short carving tool, and a handle reinforced with a brass ferrule. Most English gouges have an overall length and handle shape similar to the one shown in Fig 3.6.

Fig 3.4 Fishtail gouge, 54 × 3.

Round handle with external ferrule

Fig 3.6 Typical English short-handled carving tool.

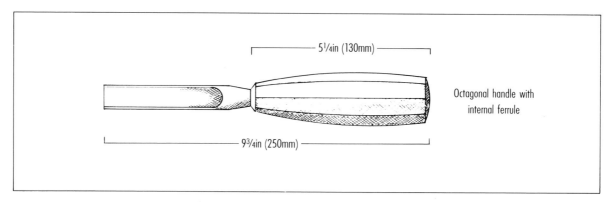

Octagonal handle with internal ferrule

Fig 3.7 Swiss-style gouge, with long hexagonal handle.

Fig 3.5 Range of standard London Pattern carving tools.

1 Straight chisel No 1

2 Straight corner chisel No 2

3 Straight gouge Nos 3–11

4 Curved gouge Nos 12–20

5 Spoon chisel No 21

6 Spoon chisel No 22

7 Spoon chisel right corner No 23

Courtesy: Ashley Iles (Edge Tools) Ltd

Swiss carving tools, which have become very popular in recent years, probably evolved because European carvers traditionally worked in woods softer than oak. Their style of carving relied mainly on hand pressure to power the gouge, with little use of a mallet, and a longer handle length was favoured. Continental carvers also adopted an hexagonal handle shape (*see* Fig 3.7), usually with an internal reinforcing sleeve.

It is interesting to note that as softer woods became fashionable, English carvers started to adopt longer and differently shaped handles. About one hundred years ago 5in (125mm) handles were common, with shapes such as those shown in Fig 3.8.

It is very much a matter of personal taste whether you buy the English or Swiss style of carving gouge. While the longer Swiss types are ideal for hand carving, many people prefer the London Pattern (English) gouge for mallet work, as the shorter length is easier to control. Handle comfort is also an important factor: some people find the hexagonal shape comfortable to use, others do not. Hexagonal

100 years ago most handles were about 5in (125mm) long

Fig 3.8 Variations in shape found in older handles.

shaped handles prevent tools from rolling off of the work table so easily, and so can prevent tools from being damaged. If you can, try holding both types and find out how they feel in use, then buy the type you like best. There is nothing wrong with mixing the styles – I have almost a hundred gouges, of which some are Swiss and some London Pattern, some are old and some new.

8 Spoon gouge front bent Nos 24–32

9 V-tool Nos 39–46

10 Grounding tool No 47 × 3 only

11 Dog-leg chisel No 52

12 Spoon gouge back bent Nos 33–38

13 Fishtail gouge No 54 × 3–11

14 Fishtail chisel No 54 × 1 & 2

The Swiss numbering system (*see* Fig 3.9) differs somewhat from the Sheffield List numbers, mainly in the shallower cutting gouges. The Swiss No 5, for example, is nearer to an English No 4; their No 7 is more like an English No 5.

Some manufacturers offer standard size tools as well as shorter (junior or amateur) versions. There is no merit at all in buying the shorter versions. Similarly, the very small lino cutting types are not worth buying – the steel is seldom tempered, so they will never hold a keen cutting edge.

A WORD ABOUT TOOL PATTERNS

Over the years generations of woodcarvers have established the size and shape of tools needed, for everything from the most basic cuts through to intricate and detailed work. The range of patterns became standardized about a hundred years ago. Most tool manufacturers were based in Sheffield, so the patterns were formulated into what came to be known as the Sheffield List. This list included all the actual shapes needed, and gave them a uniform numbering system.

You will also come across references to London Pattern carving tools. This term arose originally because, while most of the tools were made in Sheffield, a great deal of the actual carving was done in London. However, for all practical purposes the descriptions are one and the same, and you get the normal English-style carving tool. You may also find Swiss carving tools, which differ from English-style tools in the handle length and shape, and which are listed by a different system of numbers and sizes. Unless otherwise stated, the numbering used in this book (including the London Pattern numbering in Fig 13.2) is that of the Sheffield List.

SELECTING YOUR FIRST TOOLS

The size and shape of the tools you need are governed by the type and scale of the carving being

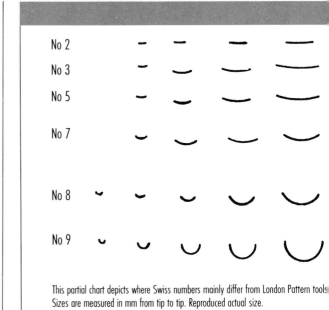

No 2	—	—	—	—
No 3	—	◡	◡	◡
No 5	—	◡	◡	◡
No 7	◡	◡	◡	◡
No 8	◡ ◡	◡	◡	◡
No 9	◡ ◡	◡	◡	◡

This partial chart depicts where Swiss numbers mainly differ from London Pattern tools. Sizes are measured in mm from tip to tip. Reproduced actual size.

Fig 3.9 Swiss gouge numbering chart.

Fig 3.10 Gouges Nos 3 and 5.

undertaken. This is why most experienced carvers end up with a vast array of tools, but for anyone just starting out a more moderate number will suffice. Indeed, it can become quite confusing if one's choice is initially too great, so buy a few tools to start with and build up as you gain more experience.

Most manufacturers offer boxed sets of tools, but because the size of a carving dictates to a great

SWISS TYPE GOUGES

Courtesy of Craft Supplies Ltd

degree the size of the tool used, a boxed set may contain one or two tools you would never use. It makes more sense to buy tools individually.

For normal size of work (anything up to the size of an A3 sheet of paper, for example), a suitable first choice of tools for beginners would be:

³⁄₈in (9mm) No 2 skew chisel
* ¹⁄₄in (6mm) No 3 gouge
⁵⁄₈in (15mm) No 3 gouge
* ³⁄₈in (9mm) No 4 gouge
¹⁄₂in (12mm) No 5 gouge
* ¹⁄₄in (6mm) No 9 gouge
* ¹⁄₁₆in (1.5mm) No 11 veiner
¹⁄₄in (6mm) No 39 60° V-tool

The ones marked with an asterisk are the basic minimum tools required to start carving. If you plan to produce carvings larger than average size, you may need to obtain some of these tools in increased blade widths.

Fig 3.11 Gouges Nos 7 and 9.

Fig 3.12 Gouge No 11.

Fig 3.13 V-tool No 39 with 60° angle.

Fig 3.14 Front-bent spoon (left) and back-bent spoon.

As you gain more experience, the following additions would be useful:

½in (12mm) No 1 chisel
⅝in (15mm) No 4 gouge
½in (12mm) No 9 gouge
¼in (6mm) No 11 veiner
½in (12mm) No 15 curved gouge
¼in (6mm) No 28 front-bent spoon bit

All these numbers refer to London Pattern tools: for their Swiss equivalents, look at the chart of Swiss carving tools (*see* Fig 3.9) and cross refer to the London Pattern chart (*see* Fig 3.2).

A ¼in (6mm) No 47 grounding tool (only made by the manufacturer Ashley Iles) is a very useful gouge for tidying up the background of relief carvings. Another tool which is very effective when working small areas of detail is a No 52 dog-leg chisel.

WHERE TO BUY TOOLS

Collecting, and using, old tools has become very popular – there are now quite a few specialist retail shops selling only old tools. Certainly these outlets can be useful if you are looking for a special size or shape of gouge, particularly one which may not even be made these days. Many people also hold the view that the quality of workmanship of old tools is superior. Two famous makes worth looking out for are Herring and Addis.

Some makers factory sharpen their tools, others do not. Clearly, from the beginner's point of view, it makes sense to buy the pre-sharpened types. The English firm Ashley Iles and the Swiss maker Pfeil come into this category. But it is important to realize that a gouge or chisel will not stay sharp, really sharp, for very long when used. You need to know how to keep your tools in razor-sharp condition. Full details concerning the methods for sharpening various tools as well as the equipment needed are provided in Chapter 4. I mention this now because if you prefer to buy a make which is not factory-sharpened, such as Henry Taylor's Acorn Brand, pre-sharpening need not be such a limiting factor.

MALLETS

Even if you plan to do most carving initially with just hand pressure, a mallet will undoubtedly be needed from time to time, and especially when waste wood has to be removed. Carving mallets have round heads and short handles (*see* Fig 3.15). It isn't really possible to use the conventional carpenter's type, because the round head of the carver's mallet is designed so it doesn't deflect the cutting line of the gouge if it is hit slightly off centre. Also, the short handle is more comfortable to use, with the hitting action coming from the forearm with the wrist locked.

Generally, mallets are made from beech to lignum vitae. The latter, being made from a denser wood, are heavier than beech ones of a similar size. But lignum vitae is becoming a rare wood, and an alternative Dutch mallet made from sustainable timber is now available under the trade name 'Lignostone'. The manufacturing process employs resin-bonded laminations to produce a heavy, dense material with similar characteristics to lignum vitae. Whatever type of mallet you buy, though, it must have an impact-absorbing handle – ash is frequently used for this purpose. A beech mallet around 3½in (90mm) diameter will be sufficient to begin with.

CLAMPS

There are various ways of holding the wood securely, but if you are starting from scratch a simple clamp is easy to use and cheap to buy (*see* Fig 3.16). You will need two G-clamps: ones with a 6in (150mm) gape will be more than adequate. For further information on holding work see Chapter 5.

Fig 3.15 Carver's mallet.

Fig 3.16 G-clamp for holding work securely.

Apart from equipment needed for keeping your tools sharp (*see* Chapter 4), we have now covered the basic requirements for carving wood. Other tools may be needed for the projects, but these will be items generally used for woodworking, and their need will be obvious at the time.

Store carving tools in a purpose-made tool roll to protect cutting edges from damage.

Summary
- Only buy good quality tools.
- Store your gouges and chisels in a tool-roll to protect their cutting edges.
- Avoid boxed sets and buy your tools individually. Start with a small number, then build up as you gain experience.
- Look out for old makes, such as Addis and Herring.

TOOL SHARPENING

To produce a perfect carving, your tools must be razor sharp. A relief carving relies for its effectiveness on light reflecting off the cut surfaces, and only sharp tools will create a really reflective surface. Cuts produced by blunt tools need extensive sanding, which leaves the carving looking dull and flat.

If you buy factory-sharpened tools you will be able to carve for a time before they need attention, and then only stropping may be required. However, sooner or later you will need to know how to sharpen the cutting edge. If your tools are not pre-sharpened, you will have to master the technique before you can begin carving.

A common mistake among beginners is failing to keep their tools really sharp because they are simply unaware that the edges are blunting. But in time, with experience, this can be felt. A cutting edge needs to be touched up by stropping frequently, perhaps as often as every ten minutes if the wood is hard – just as, say, a player chalks the tip of a snooker cue. If you neglect this, the result of hours of labour will be as if the dog has had a good chew at the wood.

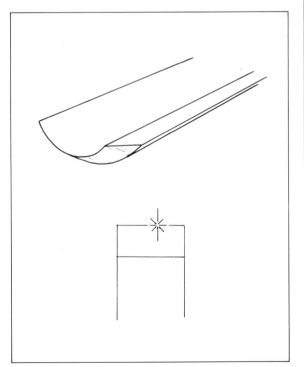

Fig 4.1 The carver's gouge has the bevel on the outside of the blade.

Fig 4.2 The carpenter's gouge has an inside bevel, but no ground bevel on the outside.

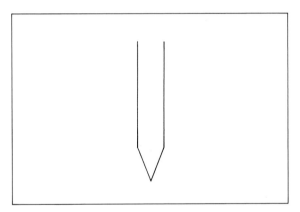

Fig 4.3 A carving chisel has two bevels.

BEVELS

When you know how to do it, each stage of sharpening is quite straightforward: stropping the cutting edge to keep it razor-sharp, honing the bevel to form the cutting edge, and perhaps once in a while re-grinding the tool. To understand each process, it is helpful to know something about bevels in general.

Bevels are needed to bring the relative thickness of the blade to a thin cutting edge. The main bevel is on the outside of the gouge, which helps to control the depth of cut (*see* Fig 4.1), although additional bevels can also be formed (*see* Fig 4.5 (*a*)). This is one of the fundamental differences between a carving gouge and a carpenter's gouge – the latter has the bevel on the inside of the blade (*see* Fig 4.2). Carving chisels have two bevels, one on each side of the blade (*see* Fig 4.3).

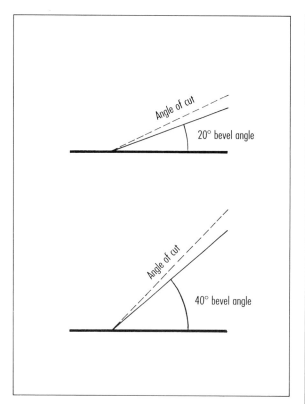

Fig 4.4 **The bevel controls the minimum angle of cut.**

The angle of the bevel is important, as it dictates the angle of cut (*see* Fig 4.4). If it is ground too shallow (say below 15°) the blade-tip would be too thin for practical use. If it is ground too steeply, entry of the tool into the wood would be difficult.

Many people new to carving experience difficulty in understanding what constitutes a correct bevel angle. Perhaps this stems from the belief that in any range of tools the bevels should always be at the same angle; a belief reinforced by the fact that tool makers invariably grind all their tools with similar bevels. If you've just bought some tools, have a look – you will almost certainly find they all have similar bevels.

In fact, the angle of the bevel should be determined by how the tool will be used. If a gouge is going to be used for working hard and tough wood, such as oak, powered by quite heavy mallet blows, the cutting edge will need to be strong. This means having a relatively short bevel with a steep angle. But if the gouge will be used on softer woods, or by hand for taking light cuts, then a lower angle of entry will be required, so you need a shallow angle bevel.

Years ago it was traditional to use a 40° angle for hard and dense woods, reducing the bevel to around 30° for softer and more easily worked timber. It was also common practice for carvers to sharpen their gouges with a narrow leading bevel set at a steeper angle than the main bevel (*see* Fig 4.5 (*a*)). Even today, this arrangement has much to commend it for gouges used for a lot of hard work, such as removing waste wood. Apart from the advantage of added strength, it gives control to the tool by allowing it to pivot at the point where the two bevels meet.

These days many carvers opt to use just a single outside bevel (*see* Fig 4.5 (*b*)), which can be sharpened easily with both mechanical systems and oilstones. However, a small bevel is frequently formed on the inside of the gouge, bringing the cutting edge nearer to the centre of the blade's thickness. This can be useful for strong tools with relatively thick blades, and has two other advantages. Firstly, when clearing away waste wood the steeper angle of the inside bevel makes chips tend to curl up and snap off more easily; secondly, it provides a better cutting point when a tool has to be used inverted, such as carving round shapes like berries or nuts (*see* Fig 4.6). You will find it useful to include an inside bevel on flatter gouges.

So, with these points in mind, let us look at how tools are sharpened.

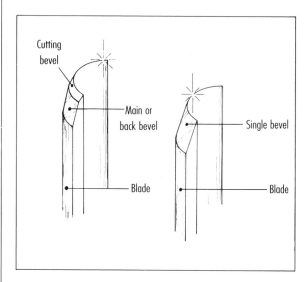

Fig 4.5 (*a*) **Traditional two-bevel edge.**
Fig 4.5 (*b*) **Single, or continuous, bevel setting.**

OILSTONES

For generations carvers have used oilstones (also known as bench stones) for honing their cutting edges. A more recent introduction is the Japanese water stone, which works on the same principle as the oilstone but has to be kept permanently wet. Water stones are also soft, and wear quickly into grooves. I prefer oilstones, so I shall concentrate on these.

There are two basic types of oilstone: man-made and natural. Man-made 'India' combination stones have a coarse grade on one side and a medium grade on the other. They are fairly inexpensive and work reasonably well. The more superior type, and a better investment in the long run, is the 'Arkansas' stone. These are natural hard stones available in medium, fine and very fine grades. You can buy individual stones of one grade, or combination types. The individual stones are better, as you can use one side for gouges, which may cause grooves, and keep the other side for flat chisels (*see* Fig 4.7).

Oilstones are lubricated with light oil, to prevent traces of metal becoming embedded in the surface. Thin the oil with a small amount of paraffin if necessary.

Fig 4.6 It can be useful to have a small inside bevel, especially when using the gouge inverted to carve convex shapes such as berries. The inside bevel also causes chips to curl and snap off easily.

Fig 4.7 A standard oilstone.

SINGLE-BEVEL GOUGE
SHARPENING (HONING)

If you are right-handed follow these instructions; for left-handed operation reverse the hands.

Apply a few drops of oil to the stone. Use the lubricated oilstone sideways on. Hold the gouge in your right hand with the index finger along the top of the blade (*see* Fig 4.8). Let the bevel rest on the surface of the stone. Position the left index and second fingers low down on the blade (*see* Fig 4.9).

Use the left hand both to press down and to provide side-to-side motion across the stone. At the

Fig 4.8 Using an oilstone – position of the right hand.

Fig 4.9 Using an oilstone – position of the left hand.

same time rotate the gouge with the right hand so that all the sweep comes into contact. You need to reach each corner of the blade (*see* Fig 4.10), but do not twist beyond the corners or you will distort the shape of the cutting edge. Some carvers prefer to adopt a figure of eight motion instead of just side to side sweeping strokes (*see* Fig 4.11). Maintain the gouge angle continually and consistently – avoid letting the handle drop at any time.

After a few strokes check for roughness on the inside of the cutting edge, which indicates when you have sharpened to the very edge of the blade. This roughness, known as the rag or burr, is taken off with a slipstone (*see* pages 42–43).

If you don't achieve this burr, check that you are applying sufficient downward pressure with your left fingers; and that you are keeping the bevel constantly in full contact with the oilstone. If you tend to drop the handle at all when the gouge is gliding across the stone it will cause the cutting edge to lift. Alternatively, you may have been holding the tool at too shallow an angle. The burr is a must.

Fig 4.10 Getting to the corner of the blade.

Fig 4.11 Using a side-to-side or figure-of-eight movement to cover the full sweep of the gouge.

Fig 4.12 Honing a two-bevel gouge, with the blade at a higher angle than for a single bevel gouge.

TWO-BEVEL GOUGE SHARPENING

The procedure is the same as for honing a single bevel, except that after resting the main bevel on the stone the handle must be raised to bring only the edge of the blade tip into contact.

Before you start, experiment by laying the main bevel on the lubricated surface of the oilstone. Then gently raise the handle until you see the oil beginning to bubble up onto the tip of the blade. The bubble is very slight, but it shows that only the edge of the gouge is resting on the oilstone. Note the angle at which you are holding the gouge, and keep to this angle to hone the leading bevel (see Fig 4.12).

When carried out correctly the cutting bevel should not be more than 1/16in (2mm) wide, and its width must be equal across the sweep of the blade. Check it does not widen at any point, which indicates unequal downward pressing being applied, or the amount of blade rotation is insufficient. Either or both will cause undue wear, and make the cutting edge become misshapen.

CHISEL SHARPENING

Chisels are honed using the oilstone lengthways on, making a forward stroke (never backwards strokes). You must use an equal number of strokes on each side of the blade to ensure the cutting edge remains in the middle. As with gouges, the angle must be kept constant throughout the stroke (see Fig 4.13). Avoid letting the handle dip to any great extent towards the end of the stroke, as this will tend to round the bevel too much.

V-TOOL HONING

Sharpen the V-tool in the same manner as for a chisel, using an equal number of strokes on each blade of the V. Then turn the oilstone sideways and rotate the underside of the tool where the two blades meet. This area should be slightly rounded like a gouge, not like a knife edge, and rounding on an oilstone will remove any small 'hook' that may form at the intersection of the two blades (see Fig 4.14).

Fig 4.13 Honing a chisel, with the blade at a low angle.

Sharpening the V-tool

Rock bottom of V from side to side . . .

. . . to remove hook
forming at tip

Fig 4.14 When honing a V-tool, rock the bottom of the V from side to side to remove the hook forming at the
tip and give the tool a slightly rounded base rather than a razor sharp angle.

Undue wear can be caused here

Fig 4.15 Honing a veiner like a gouge can cause undue wear on the sides of the U.

VEINER HONING

Veiners (U-shaped gouges) have a reputation for being difficult to sharpen. They are certainly more difficult than gouges, but should not really cause you any problems. Veiners can be honed in the same way as a single bevel gouge, but this can cause the sides to become too worn because of the veiner's U-shaped cross-section (*see* Fig 4.15). For this reason they are easier to hone if you use the oilstone lengthways, as for chisel sharpening. You must rotate the veiner so that all the sweep comes into contact with the oilstone, and avoid excessive pressure (*see* Fig 4.16).

Alternatively, use the gouge honing sequence, but do it in three parts. From an off-centre position,

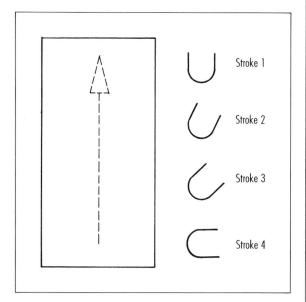

Stroke 1

Stroke 2

Stroke 3

Stroke 4

Fig 4.16 Use a forward stroke down the length of the oilstone, rotating one side of the veiner. Repeat for the other side.

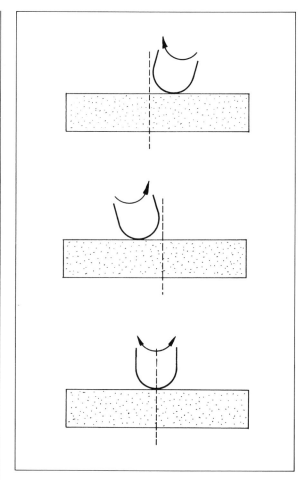

Fig 4.17 The alternative method of veiner honing is to work each side from the U-bend, then finish with a few strokes across the bottom of the blade.

where the bottom curve joins the sidewalls, hone each side in turn using an equal number of strokes. Then finish off by sharpening the bottom of the U as you would a gouge (*see* Fig 4.17).

Last but not least, if V-tools and veiners are kept well-stropped there will be virtually no need to use an oilstone.

USING SLIPSTONES

Slipstones or slips are made from the same material as oilstones, and again the Arkansas types are the better buy (*see* Fig 4.18). They are used to remove the rough burr, or rag, left on the inside of the blade when the cutting edge has been honed correctly; and also to form inside bevels.

There are two ways the burr can be removed, and in each case you need a slipstone of a size to suit the inside sweep of the gouge. You will only need a few slips, perhaps two or three, as the faces of the stones are tapered to provide edges with differing radii. Arkansas types are normally sold in sets.

If you choose to have an inside bevel, hold the blade firmly against the edge of the benchtop. With the side of the slipstone lubricated with a few drops of oil rub it against the inside edge of the gouge at an angle of about 15°. After a few strokes back and forth you will find the rough burr has been removed and a small bevel formed (*see* Fig 4.19).

Fig 4.18 An India slipstone.

Fig 4.19 Using a slip to remove honing burr and create an inside bevel.

Fig 4.20 Correct position of gouge and slip if inside bevel is not required.

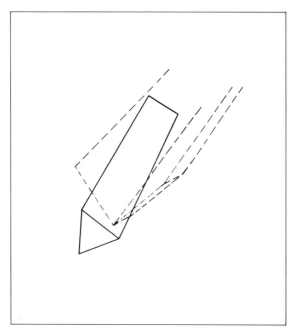

Fig 4.21 Misfitting or badly aligned triangular slips will cause parts of the blade to wear.

If you don't want the inner bevel, keep the slipstone flat against the inside of the gouge (*see* Fig 4.20).

Although triangular slips are made for V-tools, manufacturing tolerances are such that they are seldom a good fit. If you use a triangular slip, take great care to ensure you do not rub away any side wall (*see* Fig 4.21). This also applies when using a knife-edge shaped slipstone. You may find it preferable to remove any burr by cutting the sharpened V-tool across the end of a piece of coarse wood (*see* Fig 4.22). This method is also effective for taking the burr out of a U-shaped veiner.

STROPPING

When a tool has been honed it must then be stropped, to produce an even finer cutting edge and to polish the bevel. This helps to burnish each cut you make and to create a reflective surface on the carving. Stropping also restores the cutting edge between honing sessions.

Strops are made from leather with a rough surface, or nap, and you can buy purpose-made ones from craft supply shops. They can be used plain, but better results are achieved if the strop is coated with a polishing agent. Polishing powder mixed to a paste with tallow can be bought ready-prepared from a craft supplier; although chrome polish or any mild abrasive will work as long as it will stick to the leather. Impregnated strops are also available.

The stropping action is long strokes pulling the gouge, or chisel, towards you (*see* Fig 4.23). Gouges need to be twisted, so that all the sweep of the cutting edge comes into contact. Only moderate downward pressure is necessary – if you press too hard you may cut the leather.

Fig 4.22 You can remove burr from a V-tool by cutting across the end of a piece of coarse wood.

Fig 4.23 Stropping the cutting edge.

I like to polish the inside edge of my tools as well as the cutting edge. The easiest way to do this is to make polishing sticks from pieces of split bamboo cane, shaped to suit the basic gouge sweeps, covered with soft leather and coated with strop paste. Rub the stick inside the blade edge to bring it to a polished surface.

After stropping, test the cutting edge by slicing across the end-grain of a piece of pine. If the cut is clean your tool is sharp, but if the grain shows signs of having been torn, the tool is not sharp enough.

MECHANICAL HONING
AND STROPPING

In recent years a number of machines have been designed to sharpen cutting tools very efficiently.

The degree of sharpness obtained from these machines is invariably far superior to that achieved by conventional methods.

All work on the same basic principle: a rotating wheel coated with honing paste trails the tool bevel to produce a razor-sharp cutting edge. There are self-powered systems, wheels which can be drill-mounted, and others to use with a bench grinder. The machines are so simple to use that you will find little problem keeping your tools in first class order, but you must follow the manufacturer's instructions carefully (*see* Fig 4.24).

Two models are illustrated – the English 'Tyme' system (*see* Fig 4.25), and the German 'Hegner' machine (*see* Fig 4.26) which incorporates a range of wheels as well as a grinding belt. A number of other makes are available.

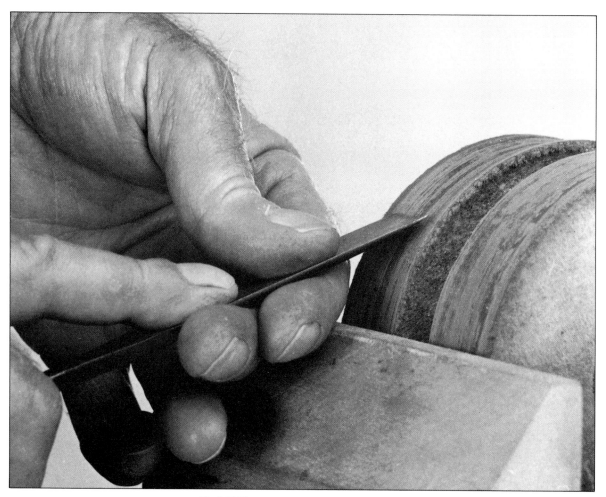

Fig 4.24 Using a mechanical honing machine.

Fig 4.25 'Tyme' honing system.

Fig 4.26 'Hegner' honing system.

Fig 4.27 Grinding with a belt sander mounted on a 20° ramp.

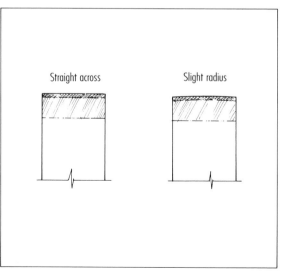

Straight across

Slight radius

Fig 4.28 Hone at right angles to the blade, or with a slight radius.

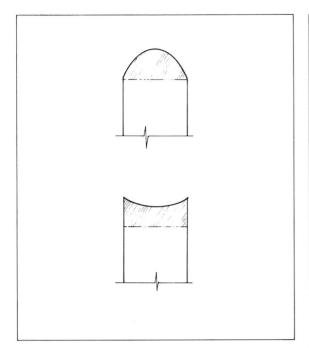

Fig 4.29 Avoid honing too rounded, or hollow.

GRINDING

Unless you are skilled at using a grinding wheel, the best advice is don't do it. You can ruin a gouge by overheating – this destroys the temper of the steel and turns the blade tip blue. Should a tool be damaged, most repairs are far better done slowly on a coarse-grade oilstone. Remedial work is always best carried out on the sides of the stone.

But if you really must grind, here are a few tips. Firstly, the larger the diameter of the wheel the better – you do not want to hollow grind the bevel. Secondly, a wet-stone grinder generates far less heat and is less likely to do any damage than a dry-stone version. For ordinary dry grinders use a 'white' wheel, as they produce less friction. Thirdly, dip the whole blade into cold water after each stroke across the wheel. Lastly, take plenty of time and avoid using excessive pressure. Always wear safety glasses.

As an alternative to a conventional grinder, you can use a belt sander as a linisher. You will need one which can be used inverted, so the belt is uppermost. Fig 4.27 shows an Elu model fitted on its stand and mounted on a ramp inclined by 20°. This gives a pre-determined level angle if the tool is held horizontally.

BASIC SHARPENING
FAULTS

A number of problems can crop up when sharpening your tools. The most common faults relate to the shape of the cutting edge, which should ideally be at right angles to the blade, or very slightly convex (*see* Fig 4.28). It should be neither too rounded nor hollow (*see* Fig 4.29). Rounding over is caused by twisting the gouge past the blade corners when honing. Hollowing is due to insufficient rotation during honing. It pays to check blades with a straight edge after honing.

Blade geometry is important because when in use all the sweep should be capable of coming into contact with the wood at more or less the same time to produce a clean cut. If the blade is misshapen torn wood will result.

The same effect is produced when the nose of the gouge is too extended. Looking at the side view, the cutting edge should be perpendicular, or lying back towards the handle – it should never project forwards (*see* Fig 4.30). The only possible exception is if a V-tool is needed to reach into a confined space, when the tip would have to project forwards. It is better to have different V-tools for specific purposes.

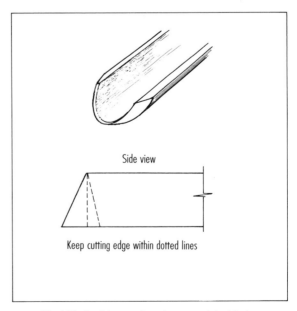

Side view

Keep cutting edge within dotted lines

Fig 4.30 Avoid extending the nose of the blade.

Another common fault is when the main bevel becomes too short, or rounded. This normally only applies to the two-bevel method of honing. Every time a tool is sharpened on an oilstone using the two-bevel method, the length of the main bevel is fractionally reduced, until the point is reached when the bevel becomes too short and its angle is too steep to cut properly. To avoid this, once in a while it will be necessary to hone only the back bevel, by placing the gouge on the oilstone with only the main bevel touching. Remedial work is best carried out using firstly a coarse India stone. This problem doesn't occur with the single-bevel sharpening method, since the bevel is extended with each honing operation.

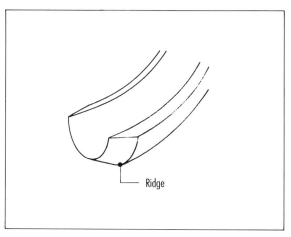

Fig 4.32 A ridge at the back of the bevel will cause a spoon to lift and not cut properly.

If the angle is not kept constant when honing, you will produce a rounded bevel which causes the cutting edge to lift on contact with the wood (*see* Fig 4.31), and gives the impression that the blade is blunt. Avoid handle wobble when using an oilstone. The problem happens less when gouges are mechanically honed.

Curved and spoon-shaped gouges seldom cut well when there is a definite heel at the rear of the bevel (*see* Fig 4.32). Ideally the back of the bevel needs to be blended into the blade. Unfortunately, manufacturers can overlook this when the bevel is originally ground.

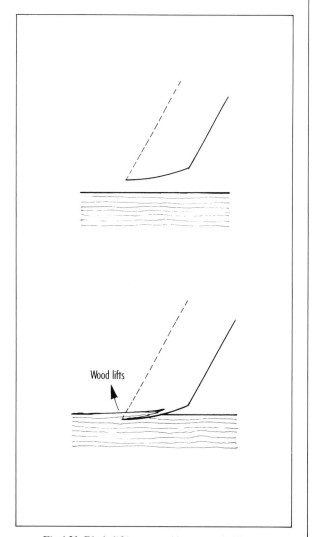

Fig 4.31 Blade lifting caused by a rounded bevel.

Summary

■ You will only carve well if your tools are sharp.

■ Check the shape of the cutting bevel frequently.

■ Store your gouges so they cannot knock together. Use a tool-roll, drawers with individual compartments, or a rack on the workshop wall.

■ Don't store carving tools mixed up with rasps, as their cutting edges will get damaged.

■ Oilstones and slips should be wiped dry immediately after use, and not left for the oil to dry on them.

METHODS OF HOLDING WORK

It is essential that your work is always securely held in place. Trying to carve a piece of wood which is constantly slipping around is both hazardous and inefficient.

THE WORK BENCH

The first step is a suitable workbench. An ordinary carpentry bench, or even a strongly-made table, will do to start with. If the bench is fitted with an end-vice and built-in fixing points such as bench-dogs, so much the better, as they will provide some firm points for holding your wood.

But the ideal position for carving is more upright than for general woodwork, and the trouble with most benches and tables is that they are too low for comfort. Bending over your work can quickly induce severe backache. What is more, most benches are too long for the average size of carved panel or plaque, and can restrict your movement. For these reasons you may eventually wish to construct a separate carving bench, as you cannot buy benches built specifically for the purpose. A worktop measuring about 26in × 25in (660mm × 630mm), with a height of between 34in and 36in (865–915mm) depending on your own height, is normally ideal (*see* Fig 5.1).

SECURING THE WOOD

The most common method of securing wood is with G-clamps (*see* Fig 5.2). The only disadvantage can be the height at which the clamp stands above the wood. On small work they can get in the way when you are carving. Sometimes a bench holdfast (*see* Fig 5.3) is used, either in conjunction with a G-clamp or alone, for holding the wood in place.

Fig 5.2 Wood secured with a G-clamp.

Fig 5.1 A carving bench.

Optional tool tray
fixed to rear edge

Concrete blocks may
be added for stability

Fig 5.3 Wood secured with a bench holdfast.

Fig 5.4 Use a frame of four plywood or hardwood strips to hold your work in place. Secure to the workbench by G-clamps.

My preference, whenever possible, is to use a backing board held to the bench by G-clamps, with a frame of wooden strips (*see* Fig 5.4) pinned to it to hold the carving in place (*see* Fig 5.5). If the strips making up the frame are shaped, oval or circular panels can still be held with ease. This arrangement allows the carving to be turned around for ease of

working, and the piece can be quickly removed when checking progress. The backing board ensures that the G-clamps are kept well away from the carving, and also helps to protect your bench from accidental damage.

Another use of a backing board is when working a very small carving, such as a roundel or motif

Fig 5.5 Backing board and wooden frame.

design. The carving wood can be screwed to the backing board from behind; shallow work can be temporarily glued down.

Some carvers favour the use of small cleats, or blocks, to hold work in place. You will need three cleats to hold one carving, and you must always protect your work with a spacer or scrap of wood set between the cleat and the carving (*see* Fig 5.6). This use of spacers applies equally if you use G-clamps directly on a carving.

Irrespective of how the work is secured, carving is generally carried out with the wood lying flat on the bench to give the greatest support. But if the work involves perspective detail, it can be helpful to incline the wood using wedges (*see* Fig 5.7) to take advantage of light cast onto it. An incline of around 60° is normally sufficient. Many carvers who do a lot of

Fig 5.6 Using cleats to hold a carving, protecting the work with scrap wood spacers.

Fig 5.7 Perspective carvings can be raised on blocks and worked on an incline to get better light.

work of this nature find a swivel-type carving vice helpful for smaller pieces, as it permits the carving to be rotated at will (*see* Fig 5.8). A robust easel is useful for larger panels. Initially, however, you will find it best to have the carving flat on the bench.

Summary

▌ Make sure your working position is really comfortable, and adjust the bench height if necessary.

▌ Consider using a backing board to hold your work, which facilitates ease of working and protects the surface of your bench.

▌ Use G-clamps to hold your work initially, then try other methods of work holding as your skill develops.

▌ Work with the carving flat on the bench, unless you are carving perspective detail.

Fig 5.8 A swivelling vice is useful for viewing perspective work.

CHAPTER SIX

BASIC CUTS

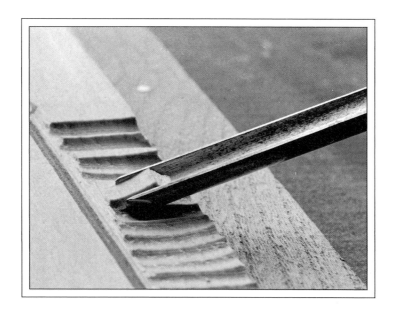

Even if you are experienced in other forms of woodwork, you will probably find it useful to practise some basic cuts before starting an actual carving.

HOLD TO HOLD A
GOUGE OR CHISEL

Holding the gouge correctly is essential both for good workmanship and for safety. There are two methods you need to know: holding a tool when using a mallet, and holding a tool when using hand pressure alone.

Fig 6.1 shows how a gouge is held in the right hand when using a mallet. To prevent the gouge slipping, the little finger can be wrapped around the base of the handle. Keep your thumb down on the index finger, not sticking upwards.

Fig 6.2 shows how a gouge or chisel is held right-handedly when it is being used only with hand pressure. Note the position of the fingers holding the blade – this provides counter-pressure to control the forward force of the cut. Also note how the heel of the left hand holding the blade rests on the wood, giving stability and assisting accurate cutting.

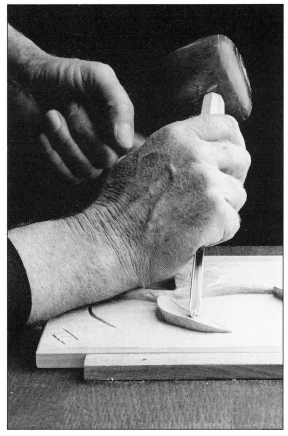

Fig 6.1 Holding a tool when using a mallet.

Fig 6.2 Holding a tool when carving with hand pressure alone.

Fig 6.3 Do not cut like this, with any part of the hand in front of the blade.

At no time should any part of the hand be in front of the blade, as shown in Fig 6.3. Make sure you always cut away from yourself, and never towards your body.

CUTTING WITH A V-TOOL

The V-tool is a versatile instrument which can be used as a pencil for 'drawing' shapes on the wood. It is also used for incising lines to mark out a relief design prior to background removal, making a straightforward V-shaped channel outside the main design (see Fig 6.4).

Another use of the V-tool is to cut decorative patterns, which are often used as component parts of designs on furniture. When cutting an incised pattern the V-tool can be twisted over to produce a slanting cut, so more light will fall on one side of the cut (see Fig 6.5). How much the tool is tilted will

V-tool trough
outside design line

Fig 6.4 Using a V-tool to outline a relief design prior to removing the waste wood of the background.

depend on how much emphasis you require. When cutting an S-bend, as in Fig 6.5, you can maintain the same twist around both curves or reverse the angle of the twist, depending on the effect you want to achieve. The width of the cut can be adjusted by the amount of downward pressure applied to the tool, so just one V-tool can be used to produce cuts of varying widths.

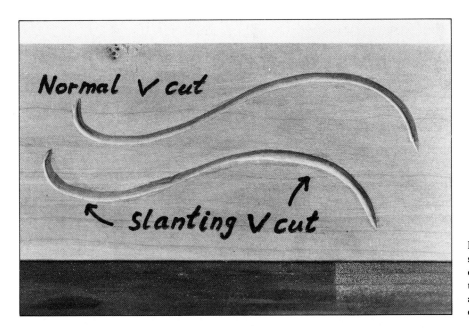

Fig 6.5 V-tools can be held straight to produce a uniform channel, or held twisted over to create an angled cut which allows more light to fall on one side of the cut.

Never use the V-tool with excessive force. Its side-walls are fragile, and can easily be snapped if you dig in too deeply. Try making some straight cuts, followed by a few curved ones.

CUTTING WITH A
NO 11 VEINER

The veiner is also used for making decorative lines, and like the V-tool it can be used for marking out patterns. But unlike the V-tool, which produces a visually hard line, the look of the veiner's cut is less obtrusive as light does not reflect off the sides of the groove so much (*see* Fig 6.6).

Generally the veiner is used to cut a U-shaped groove; it is seldom if ever tilted. There are, though, times when it can usefully be employed to sever small areas of waste wood within a design. Try some shallow cuts, and compare them with those you made with the V-tool.

CUTTING WITH A GOUGE

With all your gouges start by using short strokes. This will help you to work to a uniform depth of cut (*see* Fig 6.7). As your cutting action becomes more fluid, your strokes will lengthen naturally.

Fig 6.6 Cut created with a No 11 veiner.

Fig 6.7 Use short strokes initially to obtain a uniform depth of cut.

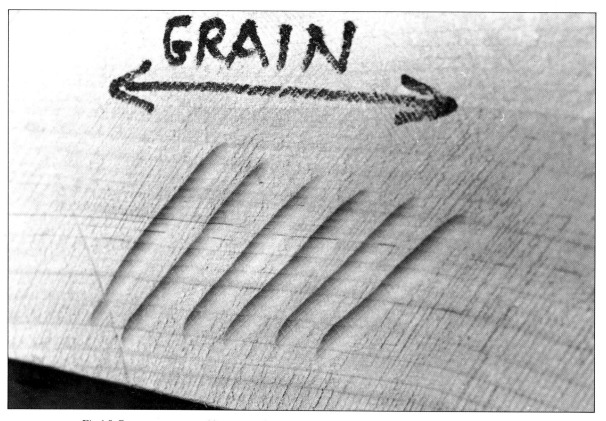

Fig 6.8 Remove waste wood by cutting diagonally or at right angles to the direction of the grain.

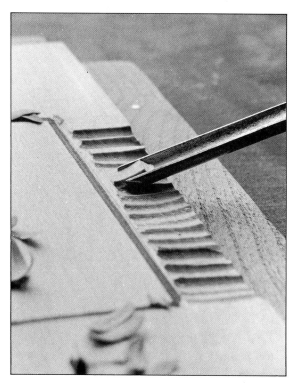

Fig 6.9 Cut inwards from an edge to support your stroke.

When removing waste wood, it is better to cut either diagonally or at right angles to the line of the grain (*see* Fig 6.8), which minimizes the chance of the wood splitting. Only when you have gained some experience is it safe to take liberties by purposely splitting off the wood in a controlled manner.

When cutting up to an edge, make the last cuts in from the edge, back towards the main part of the wood, and not from the edge out into space (*see* Fig 6.9). Cutting inwards ensures support for the stroke, which will produce a clean cut. If you do it the other way round there will be no support for the last part of the cut and the wood will break off.

DEPTH OF CUT

A gouge only works as a cutting instrument when the sharp edge of the blade is in contact with the wood (*see* Figs 6.10(*a*) and (*b*)). If you cut too deeply the top edges of the sides of the gouge blade act like wedges, causing the wood to be split apart rather than cleanly

Fig 6.10 (*a*) Cut well within depth of gouge sweep to avoid wood splitting.

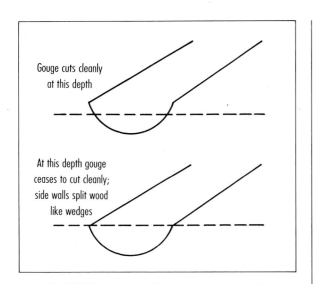

Gouge cuts cleanly
at this depth

At this depth gouge
ceases to cut cleanly;
side walls split wood
like wedges

Fig 6.10 (*b*) Correct and incorrect cutting depths.

cut. It is therefore essential always to work within the depth of cut permitted by the sweep of the gouge. This is why such a range of tools is made.

Try to avoid using the flatter gouges, such as Nos 3 or 4, when there is much wood to remove; they will only leave a ragged cut. It is best to start with a gouge with a steeper sweep, such as No 5 or No 9, then

Rough cut against
lie of grain

Smooth cut with
lie of grain

Grain direction

Fig 6.11 Cutting with the lie of the grain.

progress to the flatter ones. No 9 is a quick-cut gouge. Its sweep allows deep cuts to be made, which speedily remove excess wood. Think in terms of only ever cutting to a depth of half or two-thirds of the sweep, and you will always make clean cuts.

CUTTING WITH THE LIE OF THE GRAIN
If you make some shallow test cuts you will find in one direction you will produce bright and shiny cuts. This is when you are cutting with the lie of the grain. If you reverse the direction your cuts will be dull and slightly rough, and you are cutting against the grain. Wherever possible, and it will not always be so, try and cut with the grain (*see* Fig 6.11).

61

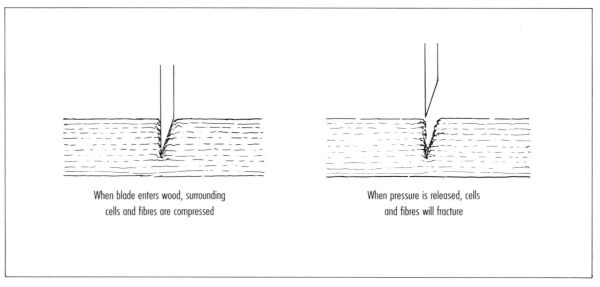

Fig 6.12 The effect of stab-cuts on wood.

STAB-CUTS

At various times you will need to make downward stab-cuts into the wood. It will happen initially when you are setting in the basic design and removing the surrounding waste wood, and later on when you model the design.

Fig 6.12 shows a gouge or chisel entering the wood to make a stab-cut. The wood is compressed by the blade thickness, and when the blade pressure is released the damaged fibres will fracture. The

Fig 6.13 Stab-cutting in from an edge to prevent the wood fracturing.

Fig 6.14 Wood splits when stab-cut in line with the grain. Make a stop-cut across the grain to prevent splitting.

weakness caused in this way can result in the wood fracturing when you do the final modelling. But if you cut back progressively to the final line of the design you will avoid this problem, as the blade pressure is then directed towards the waste area (*see* Fig 6.13).

Stab-cutting in line with the grain will cause the wood to split on either side of the tool, due to the wedging action of the blade (*see* Fig 6.14). To prevent this, make a stop-cut across the grain before making the in-line cut.

USING A SPOON GOUGE

While it is unlikely that you will need to use a spoon gouge for the first carvings you do, it may be still worthwhile knowing at this stage how the cutting action is performed.

A spoon gouge is designed to take deep cuts when hollows are being carved. Beyond a certain depth ordinary straight gouges are ineffective, but the cranked shape of the spoon enables it to work in a recess or hollow without difficulty.

The action needed to cut with a spoon is not so much a matter of pushing the gouge forwards, as is the case with the straight-bladed types, but to manipulate the handle through a downward arc while exerting slight forward pressure (*see* Fig 6.15). If the handle moves in an arc, the cutting edge will move in the opposite direction – as the handle drops the tip of the blade lifts. When cutting with a spoon gouge, it is important to think of what is happening to the handle, while observing the movement of the blade tip. It can be useful to add a twisting action as the cut takes place, which will help to sever the wood fibres.

While there is still a lot more to learn about using carving tools, you will certainly find it useful to try out the various cuts I have described before you tackle your first carving project. Use an easily worked close-grained wood, such as lime, if you can.

Summary
- Always hold the tools safely.
- The **V**-tool can be used for 'drawing' on the wood.
- Cut diagonally across the grain if you can when removing waste wood.
- Cut in from an edge.
- Take shallow cuts – don't bury the gouge.
- Cut with the lie of the grain wherever possible.
- Stab-cut across the grain prior to cutting with it.

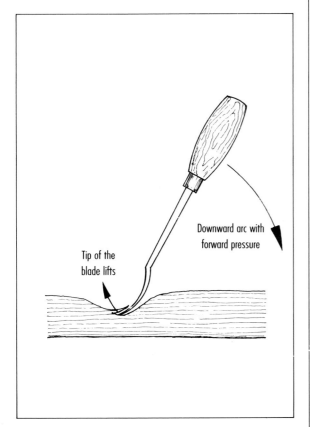

Tip of the blade lifts

Downward arc with forward pressure

Fig 6.15 Handle and blade action when cutting with a spoon gouge.

DESIGN AND DRAWING

DESIGN CONSIDERATIONS

As discussed in the introduction to this book, low relief is the most popular form of decorative carving. All repetitive designs – patterns which repeat at regular intervals, such as along a frieze – are generally better suited to a shallow treatment and are carved in low relief.

Solitary features requiring emphasis are more effective when worked deeply in high relief, which sometimes verges on three-dimensional sculpture. High relief work can be exciting, but time-consuming. Initially I suggest you concentrate on low relief.

The treatment of plaques, panels or mirrors will vary depending on the subject. There is no arbitrary figure of depth which indicates that the treatment is specifically one form or the other. Sometimes a design may call for both low and high relief: some parts of a plaque, for example, will be carved to stand out from the background while other parts will be kept shallow. In fact, the more variation a carving has in its feature levels, the more interesting it will be.

As a general rule, though, any part of a design which incorporates delicate detail has to be kept close to the background, simply because it would otherwise become too fragile. Think of the long-term durability of the carving. A deeply cut piece of work as delicate as gossamer might be a fine exercise in skilful carving, but one could question its practical use.

Start by planning to work within a depth of no more than about ½in (10mm). This will give you scope to develop depth levels and the flexibility to correct mistakes. It is far more taxing to produce a good shallow carving than one of moderate depth.

Beginners may wonder how to treat overlapping parts of a design to retain a realistic look, yet still keep to a shallow depth. But design elements which overlap one another, such as branches or stems, tend to look odd when each part is carved to its full depth. You can obtain a more realistic look if at the point of intersection the two parts are carved to half their normal depth (*see* Fig 7.1). Show that the minor branch passes beneath by dipping it to half the depth of the major branch where they meet (*see* Fig 7.2).

The project examples in this book have been chosen to build up your skill, but sooner or later you will want to create your own designs. So let us now look at some of the aspects of making designs and how to prepare drawings.

PLANNING THE DRAWING

It is vital to plan drawings with some regard to the smallest size tool you have. It is so easy to design a piece of work incorporating, for example, narrow gaps between foliage, then find you just don't have a

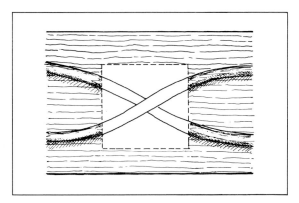

Fig 7.1 **Overlapping design elements can cause problems at their point of intersection.**

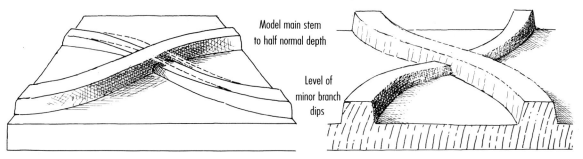

Fig 7.2 **Model overlapping design elements to only half their normal depth to create a realistic intersection.**

gouge small enough to make the cuts. If, for example, your narrowest gouge is the ¹⁄₁₆in (1.5mm) No 11 veiner, then the smallest space between parts of the carving will need to be wider than this to facilitate ease of working. There should be enough space to allow the tool to enter the gap comfortably. One way of ensuring this is to do the final drawing using a felt-tip pen rather than a pencil, as it gives a thicker line allowing more leeway when actually carving; conté-crayons and charcoal sticks also work well.

Avoid making your drawings too complicated. Too much detail can be confusing when transferred on to the wood. It helps to think along the lines of a picture painted in oils with broad strokes, rather than a watercolour. This does not mean to say you will never produce finely carved delicate work, simply that it will take patience and a lot of practice.

MATCHING THE DESIGN
TO THE WOOD

It helps if you can relate the design you have in mind to the type of timber you plan to use. This will overcome the problem of trying to carve a subject in a wood totally unsuited for the purpose. Basically, if the carving is of a delicate nature, you will need a close-grained easily worked wood with an unobtrusive grain. If the carving is more robust, the wood can be coarser and the grain stronger.

In the case of furniture carving there is usually little or no option in the type of wood. Then it is a case of making quite sure you are not tempted to use a treatment unsuitable for the wood. For example, fine and delicate carving is seldom carried out in oak. Delicacy has its place, if only to show the carver's skill, but there are times when over-treatment can be a mistake.

In the case of wall plaques, or whenever dimensions are critical, you will find it pays to select the piece of wood first, then do the design. Taken in that order you never should run out of wood. Do the design first, and you may experience problems fitting the drawing to the timber.

VIEWING DISTANCE

When planning the design think where the carving will be placed and from how far away it will be viewed. In architectural work the distance may be considerable, and the structure of the carving will need to take this into account. A ceiling boss in a church would require bold carving to be seen from ground level. But a plaque could be more delicately carved with greater detail and finesse, as its viewing distance may be only a matter of a few feet, or a metre or two. The same applies to most furniture work.

DRAWING

Build up a portfolio of ideas. Take photographs of flowers in bloom – one day you may need to carve a particular flower out of season. Both colour slides and prints are useful. You can scale up better by projecting slides onto white card and drawing around the image.

Remember that if you copy magazine or book illustrations they will usually carry a copyright restriction. Use them to stimulate your own ideas, but try to be original.

Unless there is a definite reason for using a rectilinear structure, a drawing should be composed of a series of flowing lines. (However, if you do need to produce mathematically accurate designs, Chapter 15 gives information on geometric drawing.) If you look at nature you will find that most natural shapes flow and curve. Seldom is there any angular make-up. Look at how leaves join to a stem – each intersection has a small radius. A flower stem will look more attractive drawn with a slight curve than perpendicularly. Flowing lines can also work in sympathy with the grain, or figuring, of the wood, giving emphasis to your work.

A good tip is to use 'French curves', obtainable from most art supply shops. They normally come in a set of three, and offer a wide variety of curves and scrolls. With these you should have little difficulty in creating flowing designs.

EQUAL-SIDED DESIGNS Should you wish to use a design where one side is a mirror image of the other, you only need to draw one half (*see* Fig 7.3). Turning over the paper will give you an identical reversed design.

PAPER Layout paper is ideal for drawing designs, and less costly than tracing paper. It is thin enough to superimpose two or more sheets without loss of detail, which helps considerably when building up a pattern. Just start a few sheets down into the pad and mark in the area of the wood with a broad black line. You will see this through subsequent sheets needed for the design.

Layout paper is available in standard size pads, of which A3 and A4 are the most useful. You will find it better to work with layout paper than normal weight drawing paper, but squared graph paper may be used instead.

Other aids to drawing are a clear plastic ruler, a compass, a protractor, and both 45° and 60° set-squares. Good drawing pencils and charcoal or conté-crayons are essential. I prefer to use pencil grades B and 2B. You will also need a selection of felt pens and a pack of mixed coloured chalks.

SECTIONAL SKETCHES

Relief carvings are seldom totally flat; ideally they should always contain contour features to reflect light. This means there will be low areas as well as

Fig 7.4 Flat plan drawing of flower.

high spots. To create these you must understand the three-dimensional make-up of the design.

For example, consider the true shape of a simple flower. In plan form (*see* Fig 7.4) you see the basic elements, such as the petals leading out from the calyx, the stem, and perhaps some leaves.

What you do not see, though, is how each part relates to the other in respect of contour. How, for instance, the petals curve and bend; how the stem leads to the back of the flower-head. You can apply a

Centre line

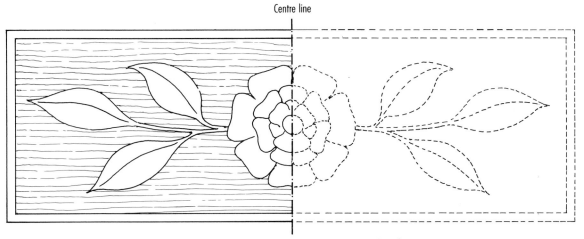

Fig 7.3 Producing a mirror image design by reversing the paper.

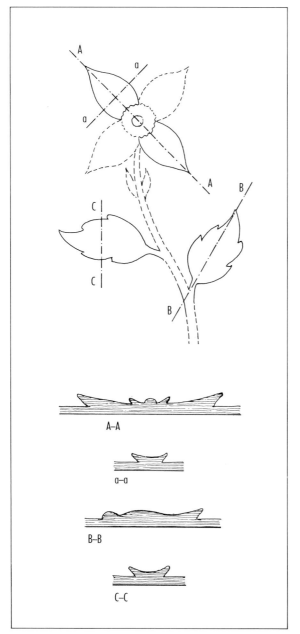

Fig 7.5 Sectional sketches through parts of the flower.

little shading, as shown, to indicate low areas, but this does not tell you how deep these low areas really are. So you need to make sketches detailing sections through various parts of the design to tell you what the shapes are like in contour and in depth (*see* Fig 7.5).

In addition to the sectional shapes you will need to consider the overall contour effect of the carving. All relief work has to be made up of a series of levels.

There will be high points, areas of mid-level, and low parts of the carving falling close to the background. It is the arrangement of these levels which will give interest to your work. The degree of variation is dependent only upon the total depth of wood available and whether you are working in low or high relief. For example, if you examine the relief design on a coin you will see how shallow it can be yet still retain some contour effect.

To plot these main levels you may find it helpful to use coloured chalk. You could use red for the high parts, brown for mid-range areas, and green for the low-lying parts of the design. All you then need to do is shade the parts of the drawing which relate to how you perceive its depth – in effect you make a colour contour map (*see* Fig 7.6). Once the drawing has been transferred to the wood you can repeat the colour shading on the wood itself.

Green Low Level	Brown Mid Level	Red High Level

Fig 7.6 Colour contour identification added to plan view of a flower.

When planning the drawing you need to ensure the primary elements follow the grain pattern of the wood you propose using. It is usual for the grain to run with the design (*see* Fig 7.7). It is also essential for delicate parts which will stand out from the background, such as leaf tips, to follow the line of the grain rather than be placed across it – when they run with the grain they will have more strength and be less prone to break off. If a leaf tip or similar delicate point falls on cross grain, keep the carving low to the background (*see* Fig 7.8).

Fig 7.7 **Plan the main design elements to run with the grain.**

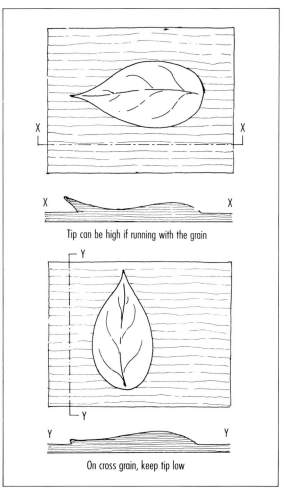

Tip can be high if running with the grain

On cross grain, keep tip low

Fig 7.8 **Delicate high points should run with the grain; cross-grain points should be kept low onto the background.**

USING A CLAY MODEL

Unless you are well acquainted with the subject, or have a well-developed sense of three-dimensional visualization, you may find you get a mental block when trying to work out a subject's contour shape. Making a clay model, technically known as a 'maquette', will help in these instances (*see* Fig 7.9).

You can use either plasticine or normal potter's clay for these models – I prefer to work in clay, which is inexpensive to buy. In either case knead your material well before use, so it becomes easily workable. You will need very little equipment for modelling your maquette: your fingers, a spatula for shaping, a small blade for cutting, a paintbrush, and a sponge and water.

COPYING DESIGNS
ONTO WOOD

Carbon paper is generally used to transfer the design to the wood, and is available in several different types.

Blue carbon paper is pencil grade, and shows up well when imprinted on to the wood. However, being soft it can smudge and it is difficult to remove surplus carbon from the wood. Black carbon paper – typewriter grade – needs more imprint pressure, which can leave marks on the surface of the wood.

Erasable carbon paper (one make is Transtrace) can be bought from specialist graphic design shops. It leaves a graphite imprint on the wood which is easily removed with a pencil rubber. Though more expensive than ordinary carbon paper, erasable paper is more convenient to use.

Drawings can be held onto the wood with either masking tape or Blu-tack on two corners. Slide the carbon paper underneath the drawing and trace over your design using a coloured ballpoint pen. This will help to avoid missing out parts of the design when you imprint through the carbon paper.

Summary
- Draw the main part of the design with broad lines.
- Use layout paper.
- Draw with flowing curves wherever possible.
- Make sectional sketches.
- Think of the contours.
- Match the wood to the design.
- Work with the run of the grain.

Fig 7.9 Use a clay model to help work out contour shapes.

CARVING IN LOW RELIEF

Fig 8.1 Flat plan drawing of carving, and sectional sketches across the contours.

Labels in figure: A, A — Half flower A–A; B, B — B–B, Tilt leaf, better access to stem; C, C — Tip to point down, C–C, Leaf area, Leaf stem, Main stem.

CARVING A FLOWER

Let's start carving! As this is your first attempt, plan to use a design of a reasonable size, which is simpler to carve.

During the planning stage you need to consider the size of the available wood. This carving needed timber measuring 7in (180mm) wide and 10in (255mm) high. Note that these dimensions form a balanced rectangle.

Choose lime, sycamore or chestnut, all of which are fairly easy to work. I used quarter-sawn lime, 1in (25mm) thick, which was then planed on both sides to give a smooth surface.

Start by making a drawing on layout paper of the design you wish to carve (see Fig 8.1). Select the diameter of the circles required for the flower with reference to the sizes of the tools you will be using. This carving was carried out with those listed as a basic selection in Chapter 3 (page 31). If the flower is too small it may prove difficult to carve, as your tools will be too big to make the necessary fine cuts. I made the diameter of the centre circle ³⁄₄in (20mm), and the outer one 2³⁄₄in (70mm).

It may prove useful to fix the petal positions by using a protractor to mark out the angles. Divide 360° by the number of petals to be drawn. In this example there are five petals, so their position at the mid-point of each one will be 72°. Then draw in their shapes freehand, using the outer circle (shown as a dotted line in Fig 8.1) as a guide. Some of the petal edges may fall outside the outer circle and some within it, depending on how they are designed.

Draw in the centre line of the stem, making sure it lines up with the centre of the circles. Use a flowing curve. Then draw in the sides of the stem to produce a gentle taper up to the flower.

When you draw the leaves, make sure there is sufficient gap between them and the stem. The gap needs to be about 50 per cent greater than the width of the tool you propose to use in cutting. I planned to cut this area with the ¼in (6mm) No 9 gouge.

When you have completed the drawing, make sectional sketches (*see* Fig 8.1). Plot the high and low parts of the design, including how the petals overlap, by using coloured chalks on your plan drawing – you could use red for high points, brown for mid-range areas, and green for low-lying parts. This will give you, in effect, a contour map to guide you when you carve. Build up your mental picture of the finished work. It is just like starting a journey: if you know where you are going, and you have a map, you will arrive. If you set off without either, you will probably get lost. Plan ahead – it pays dividends. If you wish to include a personal monogram, put it in now.

Consider the shape of the background and the style of border edge it will have. I opted for a rectangle with a bevelled, or chamfered, edge (*see* Fig 8.2). Note that it is easier to work the background to a level surface if you do not have a raised border.

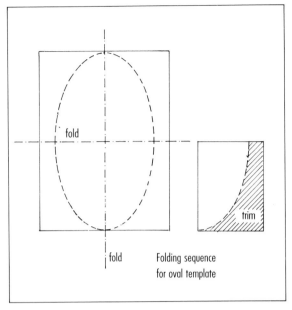

Fig 8.3 Creating an oval border.

An oval-shaped panel would need a symmetrical outline, which is easy to produce. When you have completed the drawing of the flower, simply fold the paper in four, as shown, and trim the loose edges to a chosen curve (*see* Fig 8.3). When you open out the sheet the curve will carry right around the outer edge. See pages 134–35 for more on this.

PLANNING THE
CARVING DEPTH

Plan to carve to a maximum depth of ½in (10mm) and mark the edges of the board accordingly. Slightly above this line, mark in a dotted line as a safety net (*see* Fig 8.4). Initially, all the cutting out of waste

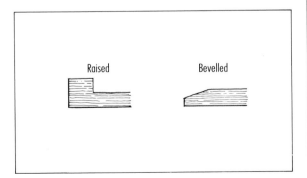

Fig 8.2 Choose either a raised or a bevelled edge.

Fig 8.4 Marking the safety net depth.

Fig 8.5 The safety net depth marked on wood.

wood (roughing out) and setting-in of the design is done to the depth of the dotted line. This will ensure that you are not left with unsightly cut marks in the final background (*see* Fig 8.5).

You may feel that the depth mentioned is quite deep for a low relief carving. It has been chosen on purpose, since it will give you ample latitude to create all the contours you need. Working to a tight, or close, tolerance is fine when you have developed your carving skill, but it does leave little or no margin for error. A very low relief is more difficult to work than a deeper carving.

OUTLINING THE DESIGN

Apply the design to the wood using carbon paper, tracing over the drawing with a ballpoint. You may find it useful to go over the outline of the wood afterwards with a felt-tip pen to give a bolder outline. Then stand back and take a good look, to see if you wish to make any changes to the design. Now is the time to do it.

Use the V-tool to cut a trench around the outside of the design (*see* Fig 8.6). Do this by lining up one corner of the blade on the drawing. The cut of the V will then be just out in the waste wood. Small areas of detail can be ignored by skipping round them. Cutting the trench in the waste wood gives you a second safety net, and allows you to remove all the surplus background without damaging the design. Whether or not you use a mallet for this work will depend largely on the type of wood you are using: you can cut the trench using simply hand pressure if the wood is soft enough, but most carvers prefer to use a mallet for greater accuracy.

Fig 8.6 Carving the outline of the design.

GROUNDWORK

In this project all the background is removed to a uniform level. Sometimes, though, relief carvings can have a dished or saucer-shaped background; or the design may be just recessed into a flat surface, like the carved stool shown at the end of this chapter (page 84). As your skill develops you can experiment with different types of background treatment.

Start removing the waste wood with the ¼in (6mm) No 9 gouge (*see* Fig 8.7). Use a mallet or, if you prefer, just hand pressure (excessive mallet force can cause stress to the surrounding wood). Work inwards away from the outer edges, keeping the depth of cut even, and cut diagonally or at right angles to the grain. Do not cut so deeply that you wedge out the wood. Avoid cutting into the design by ending the cuts just short of the V-tool trench.

As the background becomes deeper, switch over to using a flatter gouge like the No 5, then to the No 4 or No 3. This will ensure you avoid cutting through the safety net too soon. When you are making the cuts, be conscious of the texture effect which each gouge produces. This can provide valuable experience when you come to the final treatment of the background.

Getting to the point of carving the actual design can be a lengthy business if much background wood has to be removed. It is possible to speed up the process by mechanical means. A router, if you have one, will quickly remove the waste wood, but be sure that you only cut as deep as the dotted depth line. Then finish with gouge cuts to give a natural look to the carving. In many ways, though, it is better to do it all by hand to start with – you will gain so much more experience.

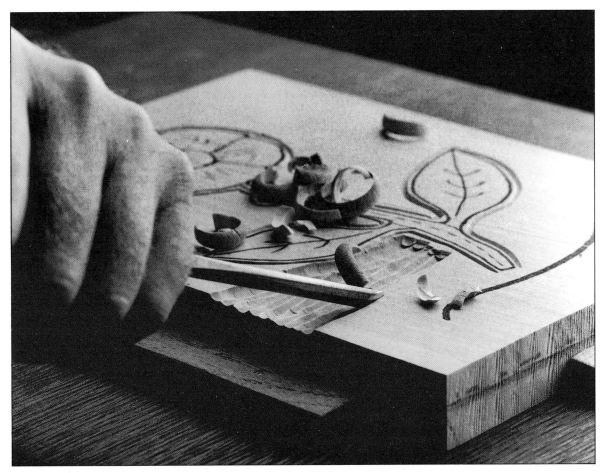

Fig 8.7 Cutting out the waste wood from the background.

TRIMMING BACK
TO THE DESIGN

When the background wood has been removed down to the safety net, the next step is to trim back to the design itself. Before you start, work out the cutting sequence to ensure you trim with cross-grain stop cuts before cutting with the grain. If you fail to do this you may well split some of the design.

Use vertical cuts back to the V-tool trench, but do not try to remove too much wood with each stroke. Keep outside the design line to begin with. If the gouge bevel is facing away from the design hold the tool vertically (*see* Fig 8.8); if it is towards the design angle the tool outwards, so that the bevel cuts down vertically (*see* Fig 8.9). Your gouges must be razor sharp, as much of the cutting will be on end-grain and the wood should be cut cleanly. The depth to which you cut is important, and you must carefully gauge the amount of downward pressure you apply.

If it is too little you will fail to carry the cut sufficiently deep; too much and you will leave stab marks in the final background surface.

Concave curves, such as those on the upper edges of the leaves, can be trimmed with the No 4 gouge. Alternatively, make a number of small cuts using a gouge with a steeper sweep than the shape of the curve. Extended convex curves, like the lower edges of the leaves, can be trimmed by making multiple cuts with the No 2 skew chisel, or with a shallow-sweep gouge.

Make a few trimming cuts, then remove some of the waste background. Each stabbing cut to trim the design and each paring cut to remove background waste have to meet cleanly: don't break away any of the wood. Work progressively from one to the other. It is not at all unusual for the background to rise up around the design area. Do be aware of this early on and remove the excess. If you don't you will certainly have to do it later, which can be troublesome as you will have to re-trim the design.

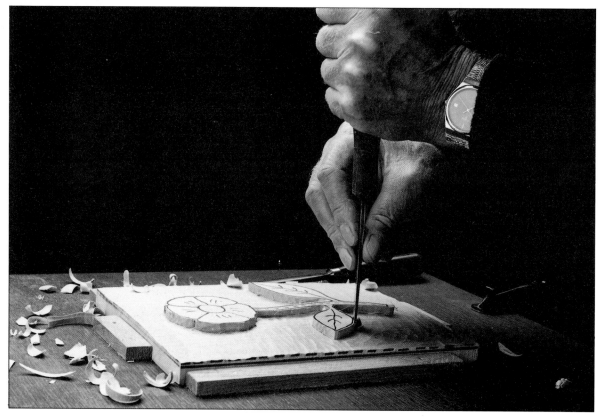

Fig 8.8 Vertical stab-cuts with the gouge bevel facing away from the design.

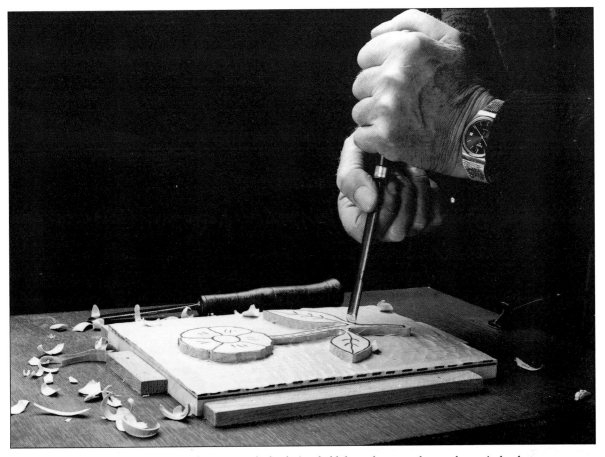

Fig 8.9 With the gouge bevel facing towards the design, hold the tool at an angle to make vertical stab-cuts.

KEEP YOUR OPTIONS OPEN

No matter how good the original artwork, you sometimes find the need to make slight modifications to the design once the carving gets under way. You may hit on an attractive area of figuring in the wood, which can be used to advantage by altering the design somewhat, or it may just be a case of correcting a mistake. For whatever reason, if you contrive to keep your options going as long as you can, you will retain flexibility of working.

This does not mean you should be over-cautious or indecisive – good carving requires positive thought and decisive action. But, equally, it does not mean you have to follow blindly what has been drawn, unless of course you are carrying out restoration work or pattern-making. You, as the carver, must have the last word on how the work is to evolve.

To keep your options open, you may not always want to cut to the drawn design immediately just because it is there. In this project I kept an option going regarding the flower stem by initially making it wide. I was then able to form the shape as the carving evolved. I might not have been quite so happy about the design if early on I had locked it into tight parameters by excessive cutting. Having wood to spare can sometimes be as useful as having money in the bank.

Another worthwhile point to remember is to let the sweeps of your gouges dictate the curves, or flutes, of the design you carve. In the early stages of your carving career, when you are acquiring the ability to cut skilfully and learning the characteristics of different woods, it is very helpful to exercise a generous amount of personal interpretation. It is for this very reason that the design of this project is an imaginary flower and not a specific one.

Fig 8.10 Start modelling at a low point in the final carving.

MODELLING THE DESIGN

Modelling the design is the exciting part; when your creative skill can be given full rein. At this point you may well wonder if you have ever really looked, in detail, at a flower or a leaf. And this is just the time to go and do so, before you start. If you can, study the shape of a leaf and a flower similar to the imaginary project design. Examine its contours; see how it curls or twists. If you use your eyes and remember what you see, your carving will be that much better.

WORKING FROM LOW AREAS TO HIGH
I have always found that if you start carving the high points first, then work through to the low levels, the carving invariably ends up deeper than intended. So I do it the other way round, fixing the low areas first as far as the design allows, then working up to the high spots.

On this project I therefore made the first cut at the top of the stem, just away from the bottom petal, using the ¼in (6mm) No 3 gouge (*see* Fig 8.10). I angled the top part of the stem on a steep gradient

to a low point at the base of the petal, to show the stem went to the back of the flower.

Having established the lowest point of the stem, I fixed the dominant angle of the leaves; slanting their surfaces towards the stem using the ⅝in (15mm) No 3 gouge this time to make broad cuts. This gave a reasonably flat surface prior to modelling the leaves, and reduced the amount of wood on the inner edges of the leaves to give better access to the adjacent stem.

The position and level of the leaf stems, joining the main stem, was then cut. For this I used the ¼in (6mm) No 9 gouge, which allowed the leaf stems to dip down from the higher levels of the leaves themselves. Using steeper sweep gouges for setting contour levels can be more effective than just using the shallow cut types, since only a small area of wood can be worked with each stroke. If flatter gouges are used all the time, the chances are that insufficient contour undulation will be developed.

Whether you work the leaves in detail next, or go to the centre of the flower to the lower part of the petals, is a matter of personal choice.

THE FLOWER CENTRE The flower centre is a dome, with the highest part being the original wood surface. Around this is a deep depression to show that the petals emanate at a lower level. The petals overlap, and have to be set on two levels (*see* Fig 8.11).

Cutting the inner dome requires preliminary stab-cuts to be made outside the circle, so the dome is not subjected to any stress as the gouge enters the wood (*see* Fig 8.12). The petals are stab-cut in a similar way, using the ½in (12mm) No 5 gouge in both cases. The same gouge was employed to cut the petal trench around to the central dome and to delineate the petal contours (*see* Fig 8.13).

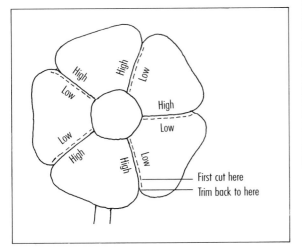

Fig 8.11 The contours of the petals.

Fig 8.12 Stab-cutting around the central dome of the flower.

Fig 8.13 Carving the petals.

Fig 8.14 Preliminary modelling of the central dome.

Fig 8.15 Finishing the dome with a skew chisel.

For rounding the dome I used two tools: the small ¼in (6mm) No 3 gouge, inverted, for the initial modelling (*see* Fig 8.14); followed by the skew chisel to perfect the shape (*see* Fig 8.15). You will need to make a slicing cut with the tip of the skew, while rotating the blade to ensure the cutting edge is continually correctly aligned to both the shape of the dome and the lie of the grain.

ADVANCING THE MODELLING Continue carving the flower with light paring cuts with the No 4 gouge to give each petal a faceted surface. (There is more about texture cutting in the next chapter, where we will consider alternative treatments for the flower centre – for the moment it is left plain.) Keep the bevel rubbing on the wood and only raise the tool handle slightly. This will produce minimal thickness cuts, and prevent the blade from digging in.

Throughout the modelling stage it is vital to cut sympathetically with the wood. You will remember from the chapter on basic cuts that if you cut with the lie of the grain you will get a shiny cut, and a rough surface to the cut if you work against the lie of the grain.

At this point in the carving you must also be very much aware of the true nature of your particular piece of wood, and especially how well the cells are bonded together. You can only ever model the design

to the capability of the wood. If you want really delicate or intricate detail, you have to be sure the wood is capable of its execution. This project was carved in good quality lime, which was capable of taking fine detail without fear of bits snapping off. Had it been carved in a coarser type of wood – mahogany, for example – I would certainly have expected possible fractures in thin cross-grain parts of the design. But even the best of woods can fracture if the cutting technique is incorrect. One common fault is to try and cut uphill, ignoring the fact that the gouge will jab into the various layers of the wood (*see* Fig 8.16).

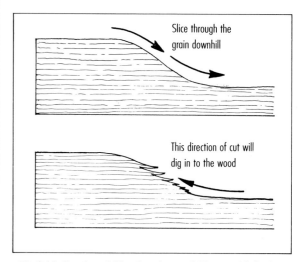

Fig 8.16 Cut downhill rather than uphill, to avoid digging into the wood.

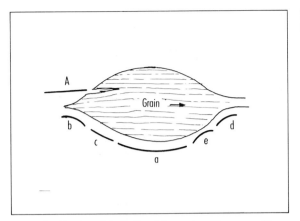

**Fig 8.17 Cutting with the lie of the grain will cause splits –
follow the 'a' to 'e' sequence to avoid this.**

PREVENTING SPLITTING When stab-cutting
and trimming a shape which is in line with the
direction of the grain, remember that the wood will
split on either side of the tool. In Fig 8.17 the wood
could split if you cut first at point A; but if you follow
the sequence 'a' to 'e' and use the sweeps shown,
there is little chance of splits. Using shallow sweeps
facing the curve helps to shape the curve, but it is
easier to cut a concave with a steep sweep facing
outwards. And don't lever out the wood instead of
cutting it cleanly away.

As you model the design it is a good idea to take the
carving off the bench periodically and stand it
upright. With some side lighting falling on the
carving, you will be better able to judge how the
contour effects are developing. Working with the
correct cast of light can also be very useful when
carving large panels in high relief, or when there are
perspective elements.

UNDERCUTTING

All relief carvings rely for their effect on highlight
areas, as well as shadows being cast. Highlights are
the raised parts, or high spots, of the design, and are
often smooth planes. The shadows are created by
undercutting parts of the design. The effect is to 'lift'
the design off the background, as well as removing
any chunky look caused by the wood of the design
being too thick. In this project undercutting was used
around the leaves and flower, with just a touch added
to the sides of the main stem.

Undercutting simply consists of removing part of
the wood which lies at the very edge of the design. It
is achieved by making downwards slanting cuts
under, for example, the edge of a leaf (*see* Fig 8.18).

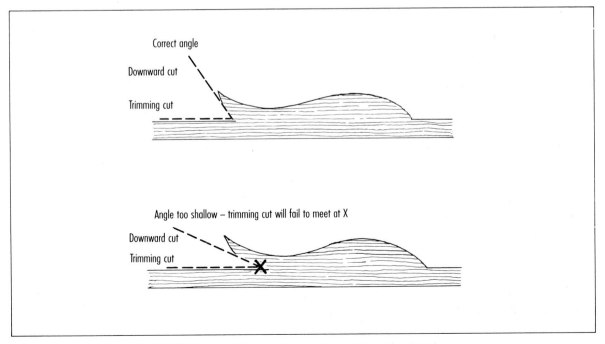

Fig 8.18 Undercut with steep downward cuts followed by trimming cuts.

Fig 8.19 Undercutting a leaf edge to create shadows.

Fig 8.20 Use a dog-leg chisel to undercut in confined areas.

Fig 8.21 Carving leaf veins with a V-tool.

Normally the cuts are made at an angle of about 60°, inclining into the underside of the design, followed by a second cut at background level to remove the waste (*see* Fig 8.19). The tools normally used are either a No 3 gouge or a chisel, depending on the shape of the design, although from time to time the design may call for a gouge with a steeper sweep. In confined spaces a dog-leg chisel can be used to remove background waste (*see* Fig 8.20). In low relief work it is a mistake to attempt to undercut at too shallow an angle, as it can be difficult to remove the waste wood cleanly.

VEINING LEAVES

The leaf veins can be cut with either a veiner (No 11 gouge) or a V-tool. Usually the sub-veins on a leaf are narrower than the main vein, which means you really need at least two sizes of the No 11 gouge. Unfortunately it is becoming increasingly difficult to buy veiners less than ¹⁄₁₆in (1.5mm) in width, and for small leaves you need to be able to cut tiny veins. For this reason many carvers opt to use the V-tool: by varying the pressure the narrowest of veins can be achieved (*see* Fig 8.21). Should the strokes look too harsh, they can be softened with very light sanding.

With the veining finished, you have the completed carving ready to be polished (*see* Fig 8.22).

Fig 8.22 The completed carving before polishing.

Polishing and other finishing treatments are discussed in the next chapter. I suggest you read about them before completing this carving.

These types of floral design are suitable for decorating furniture (*see* Fig 8.23 and 8.24).

STAGE BY STAGE CHECK LIST FOR LOW RELIEF CARVING

▮ Make certain all parts of the design can be carved with the tools you have.
▮ Draw with broad lines, avoiding too much detail.
▮ Match your wood to the design.
▮ Mark planned carving depth on the side of the wood, and dot in your safety net zone.
▮ Cut round carbon imprint using a V-tool.
▮ Remove background to the depth of the safety zone and up to the V-tool trench. Cut across grain.
▮ Trim back to the design with stab-cuts, starting outside the design area to avoid stressing the wood.
▮ Model the design using plenty of contours. Avoid over-use of shallow cut gouges.
▮ Undercut dominant edges of the design to increase the effect of shadows.

Fig 8.23 Part of some low relief carving used on a stool.

Summary
▮ Plan out your design with regard to the size of timber available and the tools you have.
▮ Keep your tools as sharp as possible.
▮ Cut cleanly.
▮ Learn to cut sympathetically with the grain.
▮ Visualize the contours of the design.
▮ Keep the image in your mind as you carve.

Fig 8.24 Floral carving suitable for furniture, carried out by student Doug Mason as a first project in low relief.

CHAPTER NINE

FINISHING, TEXTURING AND POLISHING

It is tempting to try to move quickly through the various finishing processes to achieve the end result. Unfortunately, life is just not that simple. A lot of time, effort and patience may be needed before the carving is finished. But one word of warning. When you are carrying out this work, stick to just what is required to produce a bright clean surface. Avoid the temptation to make structural changes to the carving at this late stage.

SANDING

The aim of the carver should always be to produce a relief carving using just cutting tools. By doing so the work will retain all the facet cuts, each of which acts as a tiny reflector to throw back light off the undulating surfaces. The resulting brightness is the hallmark of quality workmanship, and sets hand-carving apart from machine-produced work.

But in reality some sanding after cutting may be necessary. Much will depend on the carver's skill in coping with troublesome areas of grain and, of course, on the sharpness of the gouges used. The extent of sanding usually also depends on experience: the experienced carver will only ever sand to the barest minimum, whereas the beginner is almost invariably over-zealous in the use of abrasive paper.

Sanding papers come in various grades of grit and are made from different materials. Garnet paper is reddish-pink in colour and doesn't wear too quickly nor clog too easily. Silicon carbide papers are grey in colour and have an even surface, but do seem to wear out quite quickly. It is essential that the sanding paper you use has a flexible and thin backing, so it can be easily worked into depressions. On the back of each sheet you will find a printed number, which indicates the degree of abrasiveness – the lower the number, the coarser the abrasive. For example, 40 grit sanding paper is very coarse, and 1,000 grit is ultra-fine.

I usually choose medium grade garnet paper with a grit rating around 240 for troublesome areas, and 500 grit silicon carbide paper for any minor rubbing down. It is always best to cut the paper into strips,

rather than tearing it into pieces. Fine wire wool is frequently used to smooth highlight areas, although it can cause discoloration on light woods.

Sanding should be done in the direction of the grain, and it is important to sand with single strokes as much as you can, with the lie of the grain, rather than with a back-and-forth motion which lifts the fibres on each counter-stroke. Areas which are difficult to sand, such as where the carving has been undercut, can be burnished by using a small pointed hardwood stick (split bamboo cane is ideal) to rub the surface. This will both remove stray wisps of wood fibre and polish the surface.

If you come across patches of grain which are difficult to cut cleanly because of their twisted nature, a solution can be to sand them down smooth and then carefully re-tool the surface.

TEXTURED FINISHES

Textured finishes can adorn a carving and improve its general appearance, but if carried out with too much enthusiasm the effect can be both fussy and confused. If you plan to incorporate texture at any time, try out the treatment first on scrap wood.

Fig 9.1 Flower with sanded centre and original tool marks on the petals.

Fig 9.2 Flower with sanded petals and nail punch marks in the centre.

Fig 9.3 Flower with lightly sanded petals and chisel cross-hatching in the centre.

The completed low relief project carving (see Fig 8.22) has the background textured with random ripple cuts made with a No 3 gouge, whereas in Fig 8.24 the flower pattern has received a more defined treatment with a No 5 gouge. The slight ripple cut treatment would have been equally acceptable for the flower pattern, but the heavier cuts of the No 5 gouge would have been too much for the design of our project in Fig 8.22.

Figs 9.1, 9.2 and 9.3 illustrate how texture can affect individual parts of a design. Note that the flower centre in Fig 9.1 has been sanded smooth, as have the petals in Fig 9.2. In both cases the effect is to deaden the look of the carving. But the petals of the flower in Fig 9.1 are shown with the original tooling cuts, which have been 'softened' by slight sanding in Fig 9.3. The cross-hatching of the flower centre in Fig 9.3, made with chisel cuts, looks more realistic and indeed more traditional, than the stipple marks (see Fig 9.2) which were made with a nail.

The use of a rippling background is always preferable to a plain sanded surface (see Fig 9.4), for two reasons. Ripples act as better light reflectors when polished, and also help to disguise any flaws in the wood. The deeper the texture cuts the greater will be their effect, because deeper shadows are produced (see Fig 9.5). In this example the veiner cuts are deeper than those made with a No 9 gouge.

Fig 9.4 Plain sanded background compared to a rippling background.

Fig 9.5 Comparing the depth of cut obtained from a 3/16in (5mm) veiner and a No 9 gouge.

87

Fig 9.6 Cuts from a No 4 gouge, a No 9 gouge and a No 11 veiner, plus cross-hatching with a V-tool rather than a chisel.

Fig 9.7 Textured finishes obtained with a factory-made punch, a pozi screwdriver, and a blunted nail.

Fig 9.6 takes the example further by showing the differences between a No 4 cut, a No 9 cut, and that made with a No 11 veiner. You can also see the effect of cross-hatching made with a V-tool, which is less precise than cross-hatching with a chisel.

Fig 9.7 shows the effects which can be created with various types of punches. Factory-made grounding punches tend to give a uniform texture and are ideal for general background work. For smaller areas quite satisfactory results can be obtained with a pozi-type cross-head screwdriver, or a nail with the point blunted.

SEALING THE WOOD

Unless you are planning to use a stain, the next step in the finishing sequence is to seal the surface of the wood. This both hardens up the wood fibres (after sealing it is normal to sand lightly), and acts as a barrier against unwanted discoloration. The slight sheen which a sealer gives to the surface will help you detect problem areas requiring further attention with a gouge.

Hardening the fibres may cause some to stand proud of the surface, giving a rough feel. Taking them off with light sanding is known as de-nibbing. Use fine grade abrasive paper, such as 500 grit, or 0000 grade wire wool. Great care should be exercised when sanding a ripple-cut surface: if you sand too much you may remove all the coating from the 'high' parts and create a patchy finish.

SHELLAC SANDING SEALER Shellac is easy to use, quick-drying, and soluble in methylated spirit. It is not colourless, but has a slight yellow or brown hue which imparts a pleasant warm look to most light-coloured woods. When supplied as a sanding sealer it also contains French chalk to act as a grain filler. Shellac is widely used for wood finishing, but it is worth remembering that it is not impervious to water and can become speckled if applied in a very damp atmosphere. Its shelf life is not particularly long, and it tends to darken with age.

FRENCH POLISH has a shellac base. Some carvers use it, but its brown stain can cause a patchy effect if end-grain parts of the carving are particularly absorbent.

ACRYLIC SEALERS While shellac has been used for centuries acrylic sealers are relative newcomers. They are water soluble and extremely easy to use. An alternative to a proprietary type is satin grade acrylic varnish, which is widely available in DIY stores. Dilute it with about 20 per cent water.

Acrylic is milky-white when wet, but dries out virtually colourless, so little or no change to the hue of the wood takes place. It is thus ideal for use with very light-coloured woods such as sycamore. The only possible disadvantage is that acrylic imparts a slight plastic feel to the wood, but this is seldom noticeable when it is applied diluted. Acrylic also provides a good impervious surface.

FINISHES

OIL FINISHES Different types of oil have been used for wood finishing for centuries, but the oldest must surely be tung oil. While you can buy pure tung oil, for most needs it is far more convenient to buy a proprietary brand – in the UK, for example, Rustin's Danish Oil is widely available. If you follow the directions carefully it is simple to produce a satin-silk finish; but if you are too liberal with the amount of oil left on the wood to dry you will end up with a tacky coating which never hardens.

Linseed oil is another tried and tested medium. Usually the boiled type is used, diluted with a little pure turpentine. Like tung oil, linseed oil has a yellowish colour, and it also tends to darken with age.

Personally, I think oil finishes work best with brown woods, since their yellow tinge can discolour very light timbers. Their great advantage over other methods of sealing is their ability to work into all the small cut areas of a carving. Three applications are normally necessary. All oil treatments must be allowed to harden and age fully before being coated with wax polish, otherwise the surface can take on a 'bloom' rather akin to the look of oil on water.

WAX POLISHING A light coating of wax will enhance both the look and the feel of your work, plus helping to keep it clean. Any good quality furniture wax will be sufficient for most needs. Those containing refined beeswax cause less change to the wood colour, beeswax on its own can prove too sticky. Apply with a soft brush (a child's toothbrush will do), and work well into the cut areas. Always allow the wax to harden off before buffing with either a clean soft brush or a lint-free natural fibre cloth.

You can just wax bare wood, but it will take many coatings to build up a lasting surface, which is why sealers are used beforehand. The final finish of sealed wood can be improved prior to waxing if the surface is dressed with wax and rubbed down with worn fine grade sanding paper or wire wool. For oil treatments, improve the sealed surface by using fine grade wire wool lubricated with a few drops of finishing oil.

But no matter which treatment you decide to use, do remember two vital points. Firstly, no amount of waxing will miraculously turn a badly-produced carving into a masterpiece – the reverse is true. Poorly-cut work will stand out even more, so do keep in mind that the quality of the final finish depends completely on the skill used to cut the wood in the first place, plus the time and patience employed in preparing the work for waxing.

Secondly, aim at all times for a sheen and not a shine. The patina acquired by old furniture is the product of years of caring, and doesn't happen overnight. It takes time for oils and waxes to mature and interact with the wood resins – and naturally, if the wood has been sealed with an impervious barrier, such as acrylic, this will not happen. Science has yet to come up with a 'quick fix' treatment. A coating of wax applied sparingly at maybe three or six month intervals will be far more effective in the long term than too much too soon. Excessive waxing or oiling just creates an anaerobic layer which prevents most of the coating ever drying out fully.

Summary
∎ Spend plenty of time preparing the surface before finishing. Try to eradicate any poorly cut parts, but avoid structural changes at this stage.
∎ Choose the type of sealer with regard to the colour of the wood. Light woods respond well to either shellac or acrylic. Brown woods work well with an oil finish.
∎ Sand with care using worn fine-grade paper, or fine wire wool, after the first sealing coat is fully dry.
∎ Burnish with a hardwood stick to remove traces of fibres, especially in undercut areas.
∎ Wax is used for the final finish after sealing with shellac or acrylic, or after using oil. Use good quality wax for finishing and buff with care.

CHAPTER TEN

CARVING IN
HIGH RELIEF

The main difference between a low relief carving and one in high relief is the relative depth of wood used. For high relief you can carve wood of any thickness you like from around 1in (25mm) upwards. Apart from this the basic technique remains broadly the same. However, you must pay particular attention to the contour levels needed to create a high relief effect. Failure to do this can result in a shallower carving than intended.

Three main methods can be employed to create a carving in high relief: working in thick timber, the applied technique, or can appliqué method.

THICK TIMBER For your first attempts at high relief carving you may wish to use quite thick timber. Dramatic high relief carvings can be produced from 4in (100mm) thick timber, which gives a good grain 'flow' to the design. You could use even larger pieces, with a back to front depth of up to 12in (300mm), if they are hollowed out at the back to prevent splitting. The timber at the centre of a really thick piece will have a higher moisture content than the edges, so hollowing out the back helps to balance out the thickness of the wood and reduce the effects of any subsequent expansion or contraction.

APPLIED TECHNIQUE At one time this method was widely used for all forms of decorative carving. It works on the principle of building up the levels needed using blocks of wood, which can be pre-cut or even partially carved. When the blocks are glued together it is usual to reverse and stagger the annual ring configuration to balance out any inherent stress (see Fig. 10.1). The applied technique was extensively used for heavy and ornate work, most of which was then gilded.

But problems can occur when various segments of wood expand or contract at different rates, meaning that eventually the joints will show. The visual effect can also be marred by breaks in the flow of the grain, which is bound to happen when pieces of timber are glued together. For these reasons you may find it more satisfactory to work in a single piece of thick timber rather than using the applied technique, unless your design is particularly large and ornate.

APPLIQUÉ FURNITURE DECORATION While the building-block method of the applied technique is fine for architectural work, it is less suitable for decorating furniture, especially as heavy and ornate carving is seldom required nowadays. A simplified version of the technique has evolved for use when a deep carving is needed to decorate a piece of furniture – a decorative shell, perhaps, or an heraldic shield. The embellishment is carved first as a separate entity, and then simply glued on (see Fig 10.2).

Fig 10.1 Annual rings are reversed and staggered when building up a high relief carving, to balance the inherent stress in the wood.

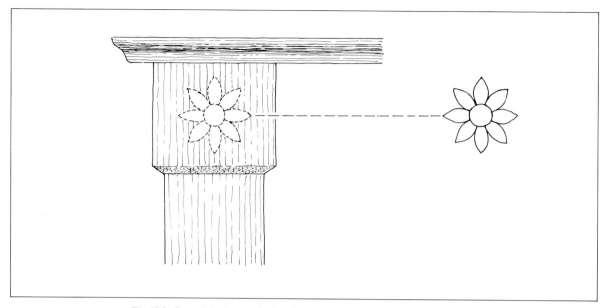

Fig 10.2 Carved design applied to furniture using the appliqué technique.

This avoids the problem of having to remove considerable quantities of valuable wood when the furniture is made, as you would using the normal relief carving method, which could either weaken the furniture or mean using far thicker wood than otherwise required. It also has the advantage that the decorative carving need not necessarily be of the same wood as the furniture, but can be stained to match. You can thus select suitable timber for both your furniture and your carving, thus avoiding the problem of carving an intricate pattern in wood which is not capable of accepting fine detail. Mouldings are often applied in the same way, just as a DIY enthusiast might use pre-formed mouldings to enhance a plain door.

The basic outline shape is usually pre-formed. The carving wood can be secured to a backing board, or to the bench, by screwing from behind – you need to make sure that the screws are in the thick part of the carving. Alternatively, you can glue the carving wood to the backing board with water-soluble glue. Sandwich a sheet of paper between the block and the backing board, or bench, to aid removal (*see* Fig 10.3). You can carve the entire piece on the backing board, or simply form the basic outline and then do the final modelling when you have glued the decoration to the furniture.

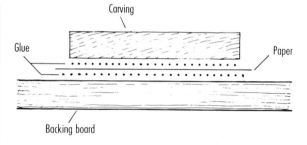

Fig 10.3 Sandwich paper between the carving and the backing board to aid removal if glued.

BACKGROUND REMOVAL

Working in high relief does, of course, necessitate the removal of considerable quantities of waste material, and there are several different methods of doing this.

In the case of a simple design it is best to use the process described in the low relief project. The design is put onto the wood with carbon paper, outlined with a V-tool, and then the surrounding wood removed by sawing, routing, or just gouge cutting. Although this can be a little tedious, especially if the wood is very thick, it does ensure that the design area is left untouched until modelling starts, and is thus the recommended method for your initial attempts at high relief.

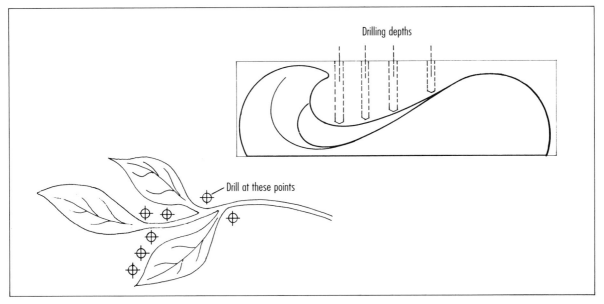

Fig 10.4 Removing waste wood with a drill, using a depth gauge to ensure the drilling ends just above the final carving level.

But as your skill increases it may help to know about alternative methods of background removal. If you are planning a more complex pattern incorporating small and delicate areas – a shield, for example, or a deeply carved flower with a number of different levels – the problem is how to dig deeply in a confined space.

In this case it is better to create the main contours first, and then re-apply the design. This usually means having to draw freehand, since invariably a paper pattern will distort when curved. But by sketching a grid of lines onto the wood after the initial shaping, you can help to locate your freehand drawing.

Another method is to fix the approximate location of the intricate parts by drilling out some of the surrounding waste wood. Use a drill with a depth gauge to ensure the holes are kept shallower than the final background level (*see* Fig 10.4).

FLEXIBLE APPROACH

Pictorial scenes may be carved better if you do not remove all the background at the outset, but leave some latitude for gauging perspective and adding to the design if required. As long as you leave enough spare wood during the roughing-out process, you will have flexibility.

For example, imagine carving a wall plaque depicting a school of dolphins leaping through the waves. Initially, you might be satisfied with drawing all or part of their bodies as seen at surface level. Later, though, as you develop the carving, it may seem a good idea to include some detail below the water-line, to expand the interest of the work and allow you to use different techniques to create the effect. You might even decide to include a sunset at wave level, or some marine creatures on the sea bed.

If all or most of the background wood is removed too rapidly, as it might be if a router is used, you could find you just have not the wood left to indulge these artistic fancies. But if you only remove the waste wood immediately surrounding the dominant parts of the design, in this example the main dolphins, you would have plenty of material available to add the extra detail.

It is thus essential to keep the design fluid when carrying out this type of work, and only remove sufficient wood as and when required. Let the design evolve as you go along. Probably much of the very ornate and complex carving of yesteryear was carried out like this.

Fig 10.5 The four leaves show the four stages of development in carving this high relief boss.

CARVING A BOSS

The wood used for this carving was 2in (50mm) thick oak. Normally the whole carving would be worked stage by stage, but in this example each leaf has received varying amounts of development to show the progression of the work (*see* Fig 10.5).

Reading from the leaf top left, the carving sequence can be followed easily. In the top left the leaf areas are marked out using a V-tool. In the top right leaf the contour levels have been set in. The bottom right leaf shows a continuation of establishing the contour levels. Note the veiner cuts on the main part of the leaf for the ridge. The bottom left segment shows the completed leaf.

Due to the narrow gaps between the four leaves, the best way to remove waste wood is to use a router. Care is needed to avoid burning the wood or overheating the cutter, which means taking a succession of shallow cuts down to the final depth of 1in (25mm). Note that if you stop the depth cutting fractionally above the required measurement, you can finish off with gouge ripple cuts.

Two other methods could be used to remove the waste wood. It can be taken out with gouges, but in that case wider divisions would be needed between the leaves to facilitate cutting. Alternatively, using the appliqué technique, the design could be pre-cut from 1in (25mm) timber.

FLORAL PLAQUE

The wood used in this project was 2in (50mm) thick sweet chestnut, and the elliptical shape of the plaque measured 11¾in by 7⅝in (295mm by 195mm). Chapter 15 gives guidance on drawing an ellipse.

MODELLING IN CLAY

After the drawing had been completed (*see* Fig 10.6), including sectional shapes, the design was modelled in clay (*see* Fig 10.7). You can make alterations easily and the model will help considerably in determining the number and depth of levels needed to create the design effectively.

TRACING THE DESIGN

The design is then drawn on the wood using carbon paper, after which you should check to see if any alterations are needed. These are often only apparent when you see the design on the wood. For example, note the difference in the width of the leaves between my original drawing and Fig 10.8, where the heavy lines have been marked.

The depth of the background was set at ½in (10mm) and marked on the edge of the panel, along with the usual dotted safety net to prevent too much wood being removed. Because of its elliptical shape, the carving was screwed to the backing board with three No 8 screws, making sure the screws did not penetrate the wood as far as the thickness of the background (*see* Fig 10.9).

OUTLINING/WASTING AWAY

Next the design outline was cut with a No 39 V-tool, working in the waste on the outside of the drawn line as described in Chapter 8. The waste background wood can be removed simply with gouge cuts, in the same way as for a low relief carving. Do not be daunted by the amount of wood which needs to be removed, but be careful not to over-stress the wood by using excessive force. Stressing the wood

If ribbon is required, allow for this when removing background

Centre line

1½in (40mm)

½in (10mm)

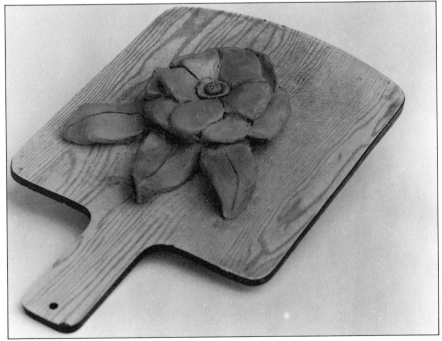

Fig 10.6 Flat plan drawing and sectional shapes for floral plaque.

Fig 10.7 Clay model of high relief floral plaque carving.

Fig 10.8 The design drawn on the wood, with heavy lines marked in to show alterations made.

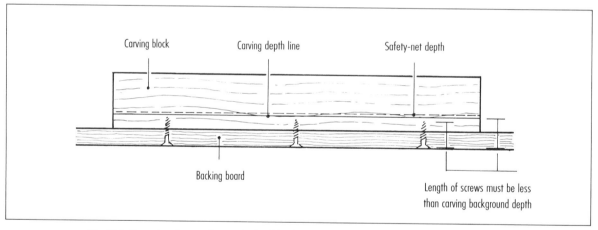

Carving block   Carving depth line   Safety-net depth

Backing board

Length of screws must be less
than carving background depth

Fig 10.9 Screwing the carving to the backing board without penetrating the background.

causes internal fractures, which may not become
apparent until the modelling is started, so just make
moderately light cuts.

Larger waste areas can be removed with a saw (*see*
Fig 10.10), but saw cuts should go no deeper than
just above the dotted safety depth line (*see* Fig 10.11).
Go any deeper than this, and you may have score
marks in the final background. Waste can also be
removed with a router (*see* Fig 10.12), against
working to just above the dotted safety net line.

Fig 10.10 Cut away large areas of waste wood with a saw.

Fig 10.11 Take care to make saw cuts to just above the dotted safety net line to avoid scoring the background.

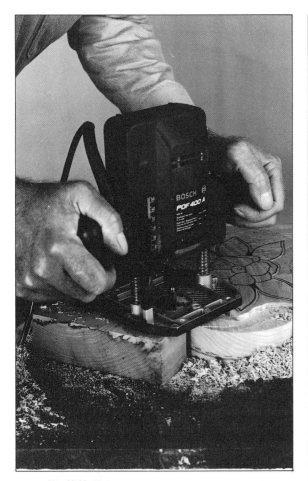

Fig 10.12 Using a router to remove waste wood.

Fig 10.13 The design is set in the wood ready for modelling.

SETTING IN

Setting in the design is done in the same way as for low relief work, by reducing the wood back to the design lines. The height of the leaves must be established, below the level of the flower. At this stage the leaves can be kept reasonably flat, so their surfaces can be cut with a No 3 gouge; but later they will need to be modelled realistically using No 5 and No 9 gouges. The division of the leaves at the point where they join the flower can be cut with a No 2 skew chisel. Set in the ribbon, making the wood slightly thicker than that which will be finally required. Fig 10.13 shows the leaves and ribbon roughly set in and ready for detailed modelling.

97

The initial cutting of the flower petals is, again, similar to the method used in low relief carving: the petals are defined with V-tool cuts on the low level sides. But the essential difference in this project is that they are arranged in two definite groups, with five upper petals lying on top of six other petals. While the clay model shows their arrangement, a sectional sketch may provide greater clarification (*see* Fig 10.14).

After V-cutting the outline of all 11 petals, fix them by shaping the bottom six petals with No 3 and No 5 gouges before working on the top five shapes. Fig 10.15 shows the initial carving on the lower petals and leaves, while the top petals have been marked with a letter H to show their high spots. You can see how the flower centre is being lowered with a No 5

Fig 10.14 Cross section showing the various levels of petals, leaves and background.

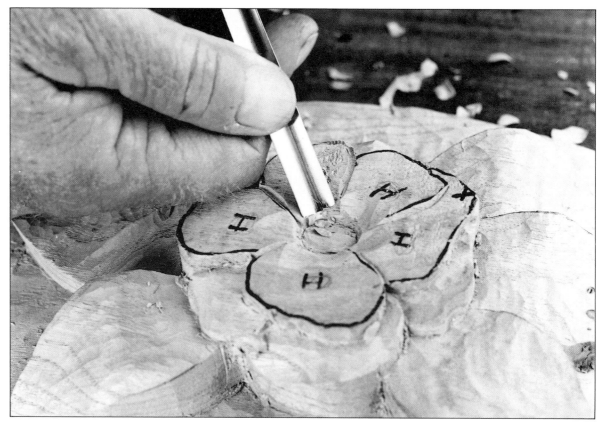

Fig 10.15 Forming the flower centre, having already worked the leaves and lower petals.

Fig 10.16 Shaping the stamen with a No 5 gouge.

gouge to the highest point of the central detail. The method is similar to that used in the low relief project: vertical stab-cuts form the central ring.

The small dome in the centre is marked in with a ¼in (6mm) No 9 gouge and rounded over using an inverted ¼in (6mm) No 3 gouge. The ring depicting the flower's stamen is then cut and shaped with the ½in (12mm) No 5 gouge (*see* Fig 10.16). The definition of the upper petals will gradually be lost as this work progresses, so set them in repeatedly with further stab cuts.

When carrying out all this central work it is essential to remove sufficient wood to ensure that the upper petals will dip in realistically towards the middle. This will also ensure sufficient access space to allow you to shape and undercut the stamen ring.

Take care, though, not to cut so deep that straight-bladed tools become inoperative because of their angle of entry. A depth of ⅜in (10mm) from the high points of the petals to the base of the central dome should be sufficient.

MODELLING THE PETALS

Petal contour shaping is done using both the No 5 and the ¼in (6mm) No 9 gouges. Cut with care, as the total effect of the carving can easily be marred by mistakes. Try to visualize the liveliness of the natural flower and exercise the maximum amount of undulation, combined with downward rolling edges in places where the tips fall on cross-grain. Moderately undercut the petals.

Fig 10.17 Starting a cut in an area of twisted grain, with the gouge blade square to the wood.

Fig 10.18 Finishing the same cut, with the blade tilted as the direction of cut has been altered to run with the lie of the grain.

By this stage in the carving you should have become aware not only of the general character of the wood, such as the lie of the grain and whether or not it is capable of accepting delicate detail, but also any problem areas. The most common troublesome features are patches of twisted or interlocked grain, which limit the cutting direction. You may well need to make modifications in the design, since these areas will certainly require a stronger and more robust style of work.

In my carving, for example, one area of the carving was wild and twisted. Not only did this mean that virtually all the cutting had to be at right angles to the length of the carving and the 'flow' of the design, but also that leaf shaping had to be done with extreme care to prevent bits of wood breaking off. I had to adjust the direction of cut frequently to compensate for the twist in the grain. Fig 10.17 shows the start of one such cut, and Fig 10.18 shows the gouge position at the end of the stroke, by which time the cutting direction has changed. At the start of the cut the blade edge is square on to the wood; by the end of the stroke it is tilted.

MODELLING THE LEAVES

Once contour modelling is under way, it is vital to stand the carving on its lower edge at frequent intervals and check the visual effect. The thickness of the wood left after the initial setting in gives scope for producing leaves with plenty of twist and curl. Avoid any temptation to retain their flate image by carving them with a gouge shallower than a No 5, and work with this tool throughout the leaf modelling to create lots of 'movement'. You will need to view the carving from the sides as much as from above to make full use of the depth of timber.

UNDERCUTTING

The leaves are undercut to increase the shadow effect, but make sure you do not cut downwards at too shallow an angle. Fig 10.19 shows the angle to use. There is no need to try to create a three-dimensional form, as this would only weaken the

carving unnecessarily. With more close-grained wood (lime, for example, rather than the chestnut I used), more undercutting can be used.

INTERPRETATION OF DETAILS

Interpretation of any leaf veining is a personal matter, and you will find it helpful at this stage to examine a real leaf carefully. Note that the veins usually lie in a shallow trench on the top side of the leaf, but on the underside they stand out. Unlike low relief work, where scope of expression may be limited by the amount of wood available, in high relief the carver should have plenty of opportunity for personal interpretation and expression.

But it is worth noting that visual impact can be lost if some parts of the work contain too much intricate detail, especially if the grain and figuring of the wood is very evident. Chestnut can best be described as a 'bold' wood with visually strong grain lines; and this grain will certainly reduce, or even negate, the effect of much minor detail. In this instance, I therefore chose to use only one central vein on each leaf.

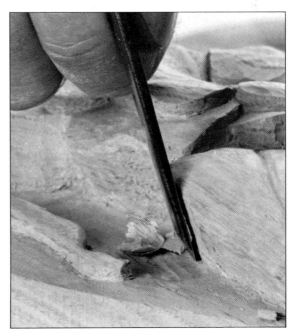

Fig 10.19 Undercutting the leaves at a sharp angle.

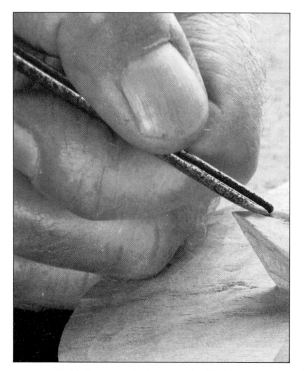

Fig 10.20 Setting in leaf veins with a No 11 veiner.

Fig 10.21 Blending the edges of the vein into the trough with a No 3 gouge.

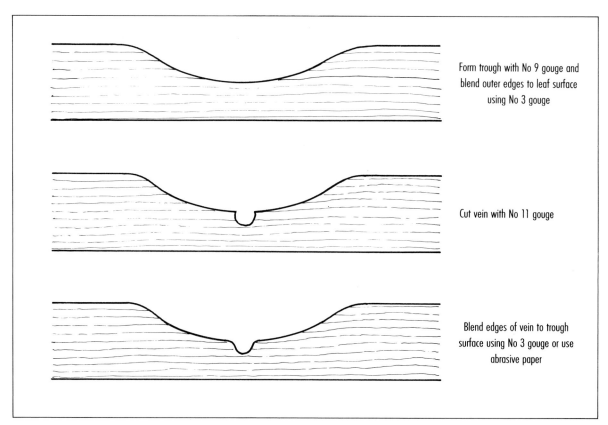

Form trough with No 9 gouge and blend outer edges to leaf surface using No 3 gouge

Cut vein with No 11 gouge

Blend edges of vein to trough surface using No 3 gouge or use abrasive paper

Fig 10.22 Step-by-step sequence of creating a leaf vein.

Fig 10.23 Step-by-step guide to carving the ribbon detail.

1 Trim wood to size
2 Draw plan view of ribbon lying flat
3 Reduce wood to ribbon

4 Cut away centre area to slope back from front edge
5 Draw in ribbon ends as seen edge-on from above

Undercut these areas

6 Trim and shape ends to blend in with central curve;
undercut as shown

The trough is created first, using the ¼in (6mm) No 9 gouge. The outer edges of the trough are then blended into the leaf surface with a No 3 gouge. Then the line of the vein is set in with the ¹⁄₁₆in (1.5mm) No 11 veiner (*see* Fig 10.20), and the edges again blended into the trough. To do this last blending you can use either the No 3 gouge (*see* Fig 10.21) or abrasive paper. Fig 10.22 shows the whole sequence of veining the leaves.

THE RIBBON

After completing the flower and leaves, work the small ribbon. Trim the wood to size and shape in block form, ignoring the twists in the ribbon at this stage. Then tilt the central portion back from the front edge using angled cuts. Finally, undercut the ends of the ribbon steeply from behind and blend them into the central portion (*see* Fig 10.23).

103

Fig 10.24 Gently removing rough areas with crumpled sandpaper.

Fig 10.25 Burnishing undercut areas with a pointed stick.

FUMING THE WOOD

As chestnut is a wood containing tannic acid, I decided to fume the carving to darken its colour. But since no cutting work is ever possible after fuming, for fear of revealing the natural colour again, it is essential first to ensure no parts need tidying up. Similarly, any sanding must be done before fuming – although only minimal sanding should be necessary if the wood has been cut correctly with sharp tools. I used crumpled 500 grit paper rubbed gently to remove any rough areas and blend in sharp edges (*see* Fig 10.24), and a pointed stick to burnish undercut areas and remove stray fibres (*see* Fig 10.25).

To fume the carving, I used two small pieces of wood to raise the carving and allow the vapour to come into contact with the back surface, a shallow container for the ammonia solution, and an old garden cloche to provide a reasonably air-tight cover

Fig 10.26 The equipment required for fuming, with a piece of natural wood placed beside the fumed carving to show the colour change achieved.

(Fig 10.26). Using a cloche, or similar clear plastic cover, enables you to check the colour change without lifting up the cover and losing the ammonia vapour. It is best to stand everything on a plastic surface while fuming actually takes place. I wanted the carving to darken to a shade similar to that of dark walnut, which took about two hours. After fuming the grain may have been raised in some areas, so sand it back very gently with fine grade paper. (For more on fuming, see page 128.)

APPLYING THE FINISH

The final treatments involved applying three coats of Danish oil, gently burnishing the wood with fine wire wool between each coat. After the last coat had dried and matured for a few days, I applied wax polish with a soft toothbrush and buffed it with a soft dry brush. You can see the end result in Fig 10.27.

Fig 10.27 The completed carving after finishing and treating.

GALLERY
OF CARVINGS

THE CARVERS

FRED COGELOW

Since taking up woodcarving in 1973 Fred Cogelow has gained a considerable international reputation and is pre-eminent in North American carving competitions. His work encompasses lifelike sculpture, incredibly beautiful relief carvings; yet despite his undoubted prowess his abundant sense of fun is seldom far below the surface. Fred brings to his work a unique and refreshing style, backed by dedicated and skilful use of technique.

In 1991 Heart Prairie Press, Whitewater, Wisconsin published his book *Sculptor in Wood*, which contains many inspiring examples, of which this picture is just one. Words can hardly describe its intricate detail.

VALERIE HADLEY

Although self-taught, Valerie Hadley has developed considerable technical expertise, which has brought commensurate recognition. She was first attracted to marine subjects and exhibited for many years at the Royal Society of Marine Artists in London. Her interest then turned to carving flower designs, and in 1986 she was elected a Founder Member of the Society of Botanical Artists. Her work, always the product of painstaking attention to detail, is in both private and corporate collections here and abroad.

ROD NAYLOR

Rod Naylor is a versatile craftsman: carver, restorer, and advisor to collectors, museums and the National Trust. He produces both carvings and sculpture in a variety of styles ranging from that of Grinling Gibbons to modern.

Like so many carvers, Rod's woodcarving career began with just a penknife and a piece of driftwood. His work now receives international acclaim.

He is author of *Woodcarving Techniques* (Batsford 1979, 1987, 1989).

PETER BOEX

A lifetime interest in carving has given Peter Boex the ability to fulfil commemorative and presentation commissions. He developed his vocation out of a childhood pastime. Early arts training, as well as solo exhibitions, have established his reputation as a skilled and imaginative craftsman whose work has wide appeal.

Peter does not try to reproduce nature; he uses shapes and forms in combination to create pieces having beauty, strength and emotion. His work ranges from expressive sculpture, through meticulously crafted decorative carvings, to pieces commissioned for church restoration.

Peter is a founder member of the Cornwall Crafts Association and has held a number of solo exhibitions.

RAY GONZALEZ

Trained as a craftsman in the field of classical and decorative ornament, Ray Gonzalez has over thirty years experience in carving and sculpture. Much of his work is commissioned, either for private ownership or for public display.

Ray is a dedicated educator, sharing his knowledge through courses held at his Somerset workshop. He lectures on woodcarving and acts as a consultant to the Rural Development Commission.

JOY FERGUSON

For some years Joy Ferguson has aided injured and environmentally distressed birds, especially sea birds. Through her rescue work, such as cleaning tar from feathers, she has acquired an intimate knowledge of bird anatomy and an unbounded wish to carve as many species as possible.

(previous page) *Clematis and Camellia*
V. Hadley (yew) 10 x 5 x 2 in (25 x 13 x 5 cm)

Oak and Laurel Leaves
R. Naylor
(limewood)
15 x 10$\frac{1}{2}$ x 2$\frac{1}{4}$ in
(380 x 265 x 57 mm)
The openness of this carving,
allied to the delicate treatment
of the leaves and branches,
are sure signs of a master
craftsman's skill. The leaves
themselves were carved to their
real-life thickness. Note the
small ribbon. Where it does not
lie against the branches it is
pierced through.

Bowl
P. Boex
(walnut)
16 x 2 in (405 x 50 mm)
Detail of a walnut bowl using a
similar design as the olive ash
platter.

Roses and Convolvulus
V. Hadley
(laburnum)
16 x 4 x 2 in
(406 x 100 x 50 mm)
This carving is enhanced by the clever use of the light coloured sapwood for the main detail to create a natural two-tone effect. It is interesting to note how the sympathetic design draws the eye upwards from the bottom of the base to the furthest points.

Fatsia and Fig Leaves with Fig Fruits
V. Hadley
(cherrywood)
8 x 29 x 1¼ in
(203 x 735 x 32 mm)
For this carving Valerie cut the wood to the shape of the design — note how each main leaf has been anchored to its neighbour to retain strength. Precise and accurate attention to detail is evidenced in the treatment given to the fatsia leaf with the main vein as a raised rib and the minor veins as incised cuts.

Platter
P. Boex
(olive ash)
16 x 2 in (405 x 50 mm)
Vine leaf and tendril
decoration, crisply carved, with
textured background.

Heron
J. Ferguson
(limewood)
8 x 12 x 1 in
(203 x 305 x 25 mm)
This low relief carving was Joy's
first serious attempt at
woodcarving and shows the
standard of work possible by a
beginner. Most of the detail has
been cut in low relief, but the
willow leaves and branches
were worked in the intaglio
method.

Ornamental Mirror Frame
R. Gonzalez
(English walnut)
24 x 17 in (610 x 430 mm)
Expertly carved in the
eighteenth century manner, the
design theme is based on a
Chinese painting frame. It
incorporates a wealth of detail
comprising arcanthus leaves,
berries and ribbons, all skilfully
and delicately represented.
These are complemented by
the natural look of the
branches forming the mirror
frame.

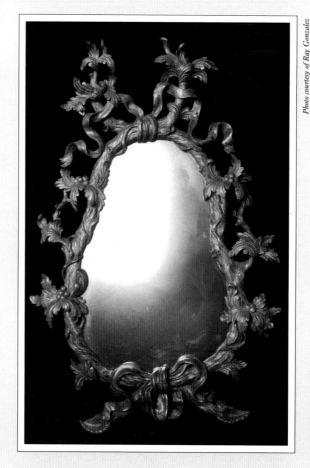

Photo courtesy of Ray Gonzalez

Satyr and Foliage
R. Naylor
(elm)
40 x 33 in (101.5 x 84 cm)
Carved from green wood
within one week of felling, then
laminated when dry. The
central figure is 8½ in
(215 mm) thick, reducing to 2 in
(50 mm) at the leaves.
  The design is based on a
Georgian original and formed
the legs of a console table.

Photo courtesy of Rod Naylor

Day's End
F. Cogelow
(butternut)
21 x 24 x 3¼ in
(535 x 610 x 82 mm)

Carved Boss
P. Boex
(brown oak)
10 x 10 x 5 in
(255 x 255 x 127 mm)
Based on a six hundred year
old Celtic design. One of a set
of bosses used in the
restoration of Lanlivery church,
Cornwall.

DEMONSTRATION CARVINGS

Low Relief Flower
(limewood)
7 x 10 x 1 in
(175 x 255 x 25 mm)
The execution of this carving is
described in Chapter 8
(Carving in Low Relief). The
polychrome treatment is
described in Chapter 13
(Colouring Wood).

Tracery Panel
(English walnut)
10 x 6½ in (255 x 165 mm)
This carving formed the subject
described in Chapter 12
(Pierced Carving) and shows
the use of open tracery work.

Summer Rose
(sycamore)
12 x 8 x 4 in
(305 x 203 x 100 mm)
Carved from a solid block of
sycamore using the high relief
technique. Extensive
undercutting was utilized to
produce deep negative areas.

CARVING RIBBONS

Carving ribbons will help you to learn about the need to have contours in your work. This example was carved from 3in (75mm) thick lime, giving plenty of scope for contour development.

PLANNING THE DESIGN

It will help to plan the design using some ribbon, or a cloth belt. Choose whatever design takes your fancy. You need to bear in mind that, in order to avoid having too much detail cut through from the underside, the ribbon needs to be about as wide as the maximum depth of the carving (*see* Fig 10.28).

Be sure to make the shape such that you can carve it with the tools you have. Both a small dog-leg chisel and a ¼in (6mm) No 28 front-bent spoon were used in this project. If these are not available then the recesses at the top of the bow would have to be both wider and shallower to give access for straight-blade tools.

There were options for waste removal in my example: the normal method of blocking in the design by initially cutting away all the surrounding wood after applying the drawing; creating the overall contour levels first before drawing the design; or using the flexible approach.

Fig 10.28 When carving ribbons, the width of the ribbon must be about the same as the depth of the final carving, to avoid too much cutting through on the underside.

Fig 10.29 The basic ribbons with the background cut away.

THE CARVING SEQUENCE

In fact I used a combination of all three. Firstly the main parameters were drawn on the wood and the background removed to half the planned depth. Then the main contours were created, which in some places obliterated the drawn design as the contour surfaces became deeper, so the missing parts were re-drawn. Finally, those parts of the design for which it was hard to determine an exact location were treated flexibly, with more than enough wood left for their modelling. The result was to retain enough wood to create the flowing curves (*see* Fig 10.29).

Fig 10.30 Using a cabinet scraper to finish off the surface of the ribbons.

Once you have done the initial roughing out, it helps to mark out the path of the ribbon using coloured chalks. This will simplify plotting the levels required for carving the overlapping parts.

FINISHING THE SURFACES

Some sanding is invariably necessary to get the curves right. Shaping is best done using the abrasive paper wrapped around small leather-covered sticks of split bamboo cane. The surface of the ribbon can be improved by using a cabinet scraper (*see* Fig 10.30), or even broken glass.

Apply texture cuts where parts of the ribbon are drawn together, and you will have the finished ribbons (*see* Fig 10.31).

Summary

▐ Use good quality timber which is capable of taking detail.

▐ Use wood 3–4in (75–100mm) thick for your first carving.

▐ Plan out the design carefully to avoid mistakes. Correcting errors can reduce the relief effect.

▐ Make a clay or plasticine model.

▐ When using a saw to remove waste, end the cut well above the final background depth to avoid score marks.

▐ Do not cut with a router to the final background depth, but leave enough wood to allow ripple cutting with a gouge.

▐ Avoid using shallow-cut gouges too extensively.

▐ Think of the contours continually as you are carving, and visualize the subject in all its three dimensions.

▐ Set in the lowest design elements as early on as you can to avoid the carving becoming deeper than planned, unless you are doing a pictorial scene requiring a more flexible approach.

Fig 10.31 The completed ribbon carving.

CARVING FLAT SURFACES

We turn now to the techniques which can be employed to decorate a surface which of necessity must remain flat. You may want to carve a chair seat or backrest, or perhaps the corners of a table-top. Normal relief treatment is clearly unsuitable: sitting on a chair embellished with a bumpy carving would be worse than sitting on a pebbly beach! In these situations you can use other methods to produce a pattern which is cut, or incised, into the surface of the wood.

INCISED CARVING

You will find examples of basic incised carving on old furniture; especially chair seats and backs, and table-top edges, for it was a popular and inexpensive way of decoration. These days at craft fairs you may well come across country-style coffee tables with rustic scenes carved in the incised method. It can be a most attractive technique, and is equally suited to producing pictorial wall-plaques.

In its simplest form, incised carving consists of cutting only with a V-tool. Just think of producing a line drawing, but using the V-tool instead of a pencil.

It is as simple as that – or nearly so, since obviously you won't be able to erase any mistakes. All you need to carry out this work is a sharp V-tool and good quality timber, and working just with a V-tool will teach you a lot about good tool control.

DESIGN CONSIDERATIONS It is better to use flowing lines rather than an angular pattern incorporating straight lines, since great care is needed to cut a truly straight line through grain of varying density. The carving shown in Fig 11.1 was worked in sycamore using just a V-tool, and is an example of the type of work that can easily be produced. If you want to carve a pictorial wall plaque like this, pick a subject which is not over-complicated and use the No 39 V-tool.

TECHNIQUE BASICS Incised carvings are normally cut using a regular V-trench along the design line. For greater accuracy it is best to work with a mallet, using light taps and taking short strokes. This helps you to cut to an even depth – seldom more than ⅛in (3mm) – and reduces the chance of the tool skating off the design and spoiling

Fig 11.1 Incised carving worked in sycamore using just a V-tool.

Fig 11.2 Typical design using the modified incised carving technique.

the surrounding wood. But if you wish to add emphasis to any part of the design, angle the tool to one side or the other to increase the amount of reflected light. This technique was used to carve the waves in Fig 11.1. Try as far as possible to cut on a shallow angle to the run of the grain, which will give a cleaner cut.

At the intersection of two lines, stop one just short of the other on either side of the crossing point. The effect will be better than if you plough through the first cut line. Your drawing will guide you as to which should be the dominant line, and the decision is normally quite simple.

Before commencing carving, make sure the surface is well prepared. If the incised lines are to be coloured, seal the wood before carving. (For further information see Chapter 13 on colouring wood.)

MODIFIED
INCISED CARVING

You can take the incised method further by using what I call the modified technique. This involves cutting the outline with a **V**-tool, then modelling the

design slightly to create shallow contours. However, it is essential not to confuse this technique with low relief carving. The background is not removed at any time, and the depth of cut is seldom greater than $\frac{1}{8}$–$\frac{3}{16}$in (3–4.5mm). Restraint must be used when cutting the contours, or you will be back to sitting on the pebble beach!

Modified incised carving has much to commend it as a means of creating simple yet effective decoration. It is an ideal treatment for timber which, because of its hardness or poor inter-cell bonding, may be difficult to carve in normal relief.

Fig 11.2 shows a typical example of the technique, suitable for a chair back, drawer front or a table rail. One half of the design could be used to decorate a cabriole leg. A floral pattern carved in this manner would be perfect for a stool top. Note that the design is a mirror image: the left portion is a reverse of the right-hand side. Only one half needed to be drawn; the paper was reversed to make the second image (*see* page 67).

INCISING THE OUTLINE The carving was carried out with a $\frac{1}{4}$in (6mm) **V**-tool, a $\frac{1}{2}$in (12mm) No 5 gouge, a $\frac{1}{4}$in (6mm) No 9 gouge, and a $\frac{1}{16}$in

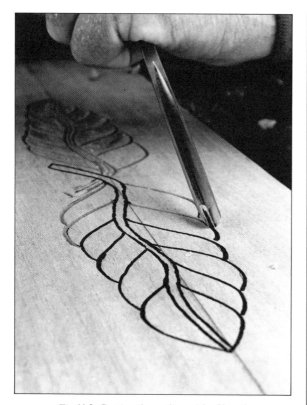

Fig 11.3 Cutting the outline with a V-tool.

Fig 11.4 The centre vein is cut with two parallel grooves.

(1.5mm) No 11 veiner (all tools included in the recommended first purchase list on page 31). The V-tool was used first, to incise all the design lines by cutting a shallow trench (*see* Fig 11.3). Note that this tool is used for incising the basic outline shape as well as each leaf segment.

In this style of carving the centre vein of the leaf is not usually shown as just an incised line, as it is for normal relief work. A better effect is achieved by cutting the outline with two parallel grooves, using a V-tool (*see* Fig 11.4), allowing sufficient width to cut a small depression along the middle of the vein with a No 11 gouge. This technique improves light reflection from the surface of the design, and is also used for stems. The effect, in cross-section, is shown in Fig 11.5.

ADDING THE CONTOUR MODELLING

Each segment of the leaves is hollowed out slightly: provided the cutting is not too deep, you can produce pleasing contours while still retaining a reasonably flat surface. These contours add considerably to the

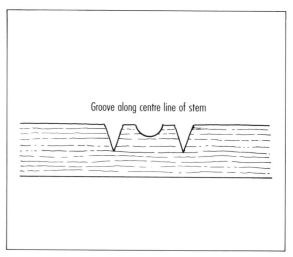

Groove along centre line of stem

Fig 11.5 Cross-section along the centre of an incised stem, showing the groove used to improve light reflection.

overall appearance of the work. A No 5 gouge is suitable for shallow contours, but when using a shallow gouge there is always a risk of the sidewalls coming into contact with the wood and causing splits. To prevent this happening, it is best to make the first cuts with a steep sweep gouge, such as the No 9, to

Fig 11.6 Each leaf segment is initially hollowed out with a No 9 gouge.

Fig 11.7 Test cut to check the lie of the grain.

Fig 11.8 Reverse the cut if the grain starts to tear.

ensure the sides are well above the level of the wood (*see* Fig 11.6). These cuts can then be blended out to the edges of the leaf segment using the No 5 gouge.

Care is needed to ensure each cut is made in sympathy with the lie of the grain, which may mean making a short test cut in one direction (*see* Fig 11.7), then reversing the cut the other way if the grain shows any sign of tearing (*see* Fig 11.8). Cutting

sympathetically with the grain flow is, of course, fundamental to all forms of carving. But whereas with normal relief work you often have the chance to rectify a mistake by lowering the wood a touch, the shallow depth of the modified incised method means you seldom find any wood to spare. Each cut has to be just right first time – but don't be put off by this, as it is good practice.

Fig 11.9 The minor stem dips on either side of the intersection with the major stem, to give the impression of one stem overlapping the other.

Fig 11.9 shows the minor stem lowered to give the impression of passing under the major stem. This necessitates only a slight change of level, made by dipping the minor stem on either side of the intersection point.

FINISHING THE SURFACES Sanding should be kept to a minimum, or the sharpness of the cut lines may be lost. You should never need paper coarser than 500 grit, and worn abrasive paper is best as its cutting action is reduced. Worn paper is also easy to scrunch into a ball for working into depressions.

INTAGLIO CARVING

Intaglio work is simply creating reversed images. You find it whenever a hollowed-out design is needed: making a mould, for example, or printing white on

Fig 11.10 Simple flower carved in the intaglio method.

Fig 11.11 Small design carved
using intaglio technique.

black. The intaglio method can be extremely useful
in decorative carving, not least because it is relatively
quick and easy. Fig 11.10 shows a flower cut with just
a few No 9 gouge strokes. In this instance the wood
has first been stained to provide a clearer illustration,
but in practice the petals would probably be
darkened.

Intaglio carving is also a good technique to use if
you are faced with carving delicate detail in wood
which is either very coarse or has lots of interlocked
grain. You can only ever carve to the capability of the
timber, and in these circumstances the chances are
that sooner or later parts of the design will split and
break off if you use the normal relief technique. But
if you use the intaglio method the design is switched
to a negative image, so the high parts of the design
become low parts, and there are no delicate high-
level details to snap off.

TOOLS AND TECHNIQUE Fig 11.11 shows a
simple yet effective way of producing delicate detail
which is too small for carving in relief in coarse
wood. The example was cut with just a V-tool. This
treatment can be incorporated into other styles of
carving if you are ever in any doubt about the
capability of the wood to accept fine detail in raised

relief. It can be useful should you ever wish to carve
an outdoor sign, as rain will run off better than off a
raised relief.

Just as with the modified incised technique,
careful and precise cutting is vital in intaglio carving.
Figs 11.12 and 11.13 show the flat plan of a leaf to be
carved, and the initial cutting sequence. Note that
the No 11 veiner is used for the outlining stage: the
round-bottomed cut of the veiner is easier to blend
into the leaf shape than the sharp cut of a V-tool.
Remember to cut *inside* the design lines.

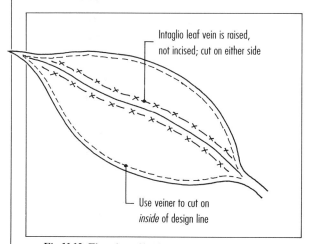

Fig 11.12 Flat plan of leaf to be carved in the intaglio
method.

Intaglio leaf vein is raised,
not incised; cut on either side

Use veiner to cut on
inside of design line

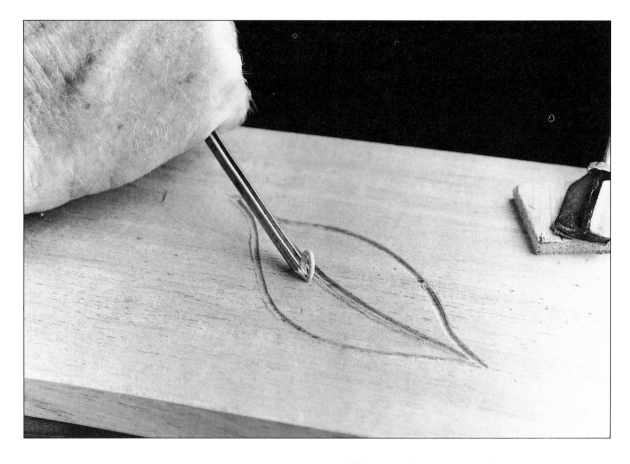

Fig 11.13 Use a veiner to outline an intaglio design before cutting the main wood with gouges.

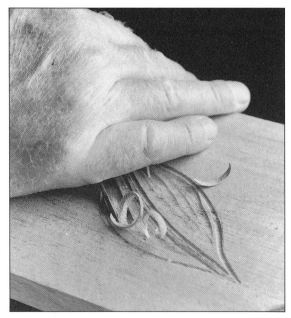

Fig 11.14 Forming the main depressions in the leaf with a No 9 gouge.

The main depressions are formed with a steep sweep gouge, such as a No 9, so the blade edges do not tear out any wood (*see* Fig 11.14). If you carve carefully you can achieve quite an even surface; any remaining marks will provide useful texture, so little or no sanding should be needed (*see* Fig 11.15). Only straight-bladed tools are normally required for intaglio cutting on flat surfaces. Try to avoid a design involving really deep impressions unless you have spoon-shaped gouges.

Fig 11.16 shows the final leaf carved as a reverse image in the wood, and can also illustrate a curious aspect of intaglio work. Depending on how the light falls on its surface, the carving may have a trompe l'oeil effect of appearing to protrude from the surface of the wood rather than being recessed into it. You may even have difficulty in 'reading' the photographs of intaglio work in this book as being recessed rather than raised carvings. It is simply a trick of the light, and turning the book upside down may help you to see the reversed image.

Fig 11.15 Shallow gouge marks are left to give texture to the carving.

Fig 11.16 The finished intaglio carved leaf.

Fig 11.17 Sequence of cuts used in chip carving.

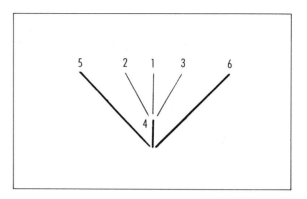

Fig 11.18 Typical traditional chip carved design.

Slice to remove after stab-cuts 1, 2 and 3

A Draw 3 concentric circles
B Decide number of segments and divide into 360 to calculate angle
C Mark in tips of segments
D Stab-cut outline of tips and along short segment lines
E Using No 3 gouge, remove waste to outer circle
F Stab-cut troughs deeper at front; angle-cut facets; inner circle can be rounded over

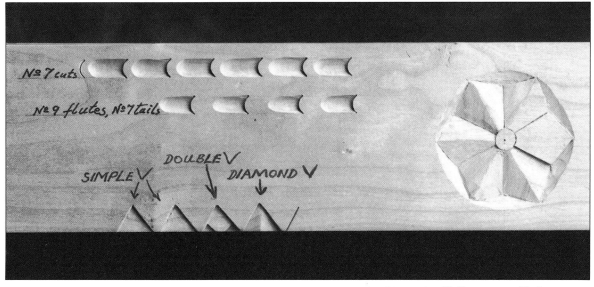

Fig 11.19 A simple chip carved flower, and five types of borders cut by chip carving: No 7 gouge cuts; No 9 flutes and No 7 tails; simple V; double V; and diamond V.

CHIP CARVING

The technique of cutting designs with defined angles has been widely used for centuries. Historians attribute its origin in the western world to parts of Scandinavia, although similar methods were clearly used by primitive man in many other areas. During the latter part of the last century chip carving became very popular. It was a favourite hobby for Victorian ladies to decorate box lids in this way, or in fact any small wooden article capable of being carved by hand with geometric designs.

TOOLS AND TECHNIQUE Serious chip carvers use special knives, but quite reasonable results can be achieved with a skew chisel. A V-tool with a long point is also used for clearing waste wood from crevices.

The basic principle of chip carving is very much the same as that used for cutting notches in a stick with a penknife. Firstly a downward cut is made, followed by angled cuts on either side (*see* Fig 11.17) to make intricate patterns. Fig 11.18 illustrates a typical traditional design, executed in simple form in Fig 11.19. Fig 11.19 also shows three examples of how chip carving patterns are useful for decorating borders.

Summary

■ Use the incised method for table and chair decorations, or whenever the surrounding surface needs to be kept flat, or when you simply need to 'draw' in the wood.

■ Use the modified incised method for better light reflection.

■ Use the intaglio style when the detail to be worked is too small or delicate for the wood to accept other carving methods, or when you want to produce a simple design quickly.

■ Keep to simple designs for all three techniques, as they are much easier to work.

■ Plan your cutting sequence before you start, as with all three methods you will have little chance of correcting mistakes.

■ Try not to be over-ambitious, and avoid working to too great a depth.

■ Work in sympathy with the wood, going with the lie of the grain for bright, clean cuts.

■ Chip carving makes simple border patterns which can be used with effect on furniture.

■ Make sure your tools are really sharp. All these styles suffer in appearance if they have been heavily sanded.

CHAPTER TWELVE

PIERCED CARVING

The essence of pierced work is to produce tracery with a sense or feeling of spacial lightness. It is impossible to achieve the same degree of effect with other forms of decorative carving.

This type of work used to be very popular. You will find beautiful examples of pierced carving in old churches, where the technique was used to fashion rood screens of considerable delicacy. Similarly, for centuries the pierced method has been widely used by Indian carvers for both temple and house decoration. It is a style which should not be overlooked by any aspiring woodcarver. The technique is not as difficult as it may first appear. Even a simple design will teach you about cutting wood delicately, and it can be tremendously satisfying.

PROJECT

WALL PLAQUE IN PIERCED CARVING

The example used here (see the last page of colour section) to illustrate the main points of pierced carving was designed as a wall plaque, where the colour and texture of the wall itself will be visible through the pierced areas. An attractive variation is to back the carving with mirror glass.

WOOD SELECTION

You need to be very selective in the type of wood you use. It must be stable, well seasoned, and certainly close-grained: lime, sycamore and walnut are ideal. Unless you have a specific requirement, keep to a prepared thickness of about ¾in (20mm), as beyond this too much of the underside of the carving can become visible.

DESIGN

Choose a fairly simple design for your first attempt. Lots of interlacing elements may look all very well on paper, but can be exasperating to carve. As with other types of carving, plan your design with some reference to the sizes of your tools.

Fig 12.1 Starting to remove waste wood from a pierced carving, leaving elements like stems oversized to allow freedom in final placing.

Much of the pierced effect is obtained from the shapes of the cutout, or negative, parts of the design. When drawing it is worthwhile shading or hatching these areas to see how they look. You could have both positive and negative leaf shapes, for example, which works well on bold patterns but can tend to give a confused impression if too repetitive.

At all times keep in mind the practicalities of cutting and shaping the wood. A successful pierced carving needs sufficient in-built strength, and there is little merit in making the design so delicate that the carving is impossible to finish. Once you have the carbon imprint on the wood, make sure you are entirely happy with the design. Look at the thickness of interlocking parts which lie on the cross-grain, and avoid making them too slender. Note how the stems used in the example are oversized, to give some freedom when deciding their final position and shape.

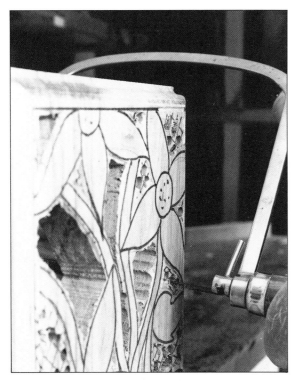

Fig 12.2 Removing waste wood with a coping saw.

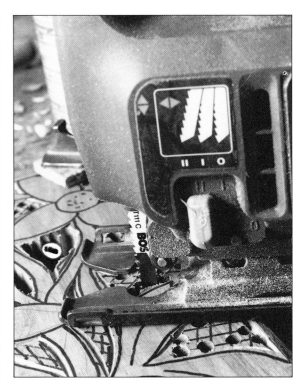

Fig 12.3 Removing waste wood with a jigsaw.

OUTLINING AND
REMOVING NEGATIVE
SPACES

Take the precaution of cutting around the whole design with a V-tool to create a safety net before starting to remove waste from each negative space (*see* Fig 12.1). You can use a coping saw to create the voids (*see* Fig 12.2) by first drilling multiple holes close to the V-line. Make sure you keep the drill perpendicular and that you do not stray into any of the design. Alternatively a jigsaw can be used (*see* Fig 12.3), in which case you may not need to drill quite so many holes.

Once the waste has been removed, trim the spaces back to the drawn lines of the design. If you use a gouge (*see* Fig 12.4), do not use excessive force. This technique calls for a delicate touch and razor sharp tools, and the neater your work at this stage the better. It is also possible to carry out some or all of this work using a rasp. Whichever way you choose to do it, keep the sides of the design as vertical as you

Fig 12.4 Cutting back to the lines of the design with a gouge.

120

can, and check your progress regularly from different viewpoints. If you are in any doubt, just leave a little extra wood in place and make the final adjustment later.

This next stage is similar to any low or high relief carving. Do it with coloured chalk if you wish, as described previously (*see* page 68). Avoid keeping all the design on the original surface level – the effect will be too flat. Plot the depths and mark the sides of the design accordingly. If the carving is to be viewed from both front and back (double-sided), you will need to plot both sets of contours. In the low areas only cut away about three-quarters of the excess wood (you still have work to do on the back of the carving). Much of this can usually be done with a skew chisel, and its slicing action will assist cutting against the lie of the grain. When using a gouge (*see* Fig 12.5) try to adopt the habit of using a slight twisting action, which reduces the pressure on the wood.

Fig 12.5 Using a gouge to cut down to low-lying areas.

Fig 12.6 Roughly modelling high parts of the design with a gouge.

MODELLING

Then start to model roughly all the high-lying parts (*see* Fig 12.6), keeping low parts in block form or they may become too weak. Use centre lines to finalize the position of narrower elements (*see* Fig 12.7).

UNDERCUTTING

Once you have set in the design to approximately the depths you require, you can remove the surplus wood from the back of a single-sided carving. The extent of undercutting will depend on how you want the carving to ultimately be viewed. For example, if the carving is only to be seen from some distance you will not require a great degree of delicacy. But if viewed from just a few paces, more refined treatment will be called for. Undercutting means removing wood from the outer edges of the design at a fairly steep angle (*see* pages 81–83), and in pierced carving is known as feather-edging.

Fig 12.7 Mark centre lines to establish the final position of narrow elements such as stems.

SHAPING FROM THE BACK

Some shaping from the back will be necessary, or there will be a disproportionate difference in thickness between the low and high areas. It is not necessary to think in true three-dimensional terms, as this could cause the carving to become structurally very weak. All that is ever needed is to feather-edge wider surfaces, such as leaves and petals, and to give the stems and branches a flat-bottomed oval sectional shape. A rasp or small riffler file will help in difficult areas (*see* Fig 12.8); another useful tool is a rotary cutter fitted to the drive of a miniature drill (*see* Fig 12.9). Again, regularly check progress by standing the carving up and viewing it from different angles.

Generally, both undercutting and shaping from the back are carried out as one operation.

Fig 12.8 Using a riffler file to feather-edge the back of a single-sided carving.

Fig 12.9 A rotary cutter fitted to a miniature drill is useful for feather-edging.

COMPLETING THE
CARVING

Once you have cleared away the surplus wood from the rear, turn the carving over and finish the front modelling. After this stage you may find there is still some wood at the back requiring attention, but make sure you don't get carried away and cut with too much enthusiasm. At this stage you will not have much, if any, spare wood left to correct mistakes.

Fig 12.10 shows the carving nearing completion. Note how the intertwining stems have been left with plenty of inherent strength to support the remainder of the design, yet by undercutting their scale is compatible with the flowers.

Fig 12.10 The carving nears completion, with only a small amount of tidying up left to be done.

Summary
▮ Choose the design with some reference to the effect created by the negative voids. If you wish, relate spaces to positive elements.
▮ Make sure there is strength to the design, but aim to give the carving a feeling of lightness.
▮ Use stable, close-grained wood which is not too hard.
▮ Make sure you work in the waste wood outside the V-trench before cutting out negative parts.
▮ Avoid using too much force, as this could damage the structure. Carve with a light touch.
▮ Repeatedly check progress from different viewpoints.

COLOURING
WOOD

Carvings are generally left showing the natural colour and figuring of the wood, but in certain situations some timbers can appear too bland and uninteresting. What is more, if the carving is to be applied to a piece of furniture there may be considerable mismatch of colour tone. For either of these reasons you may want to colour the wood.

The colouring of wood is by no means a new idea. From earliest times ochres, earth pigments, herbs and other wild plants have been used as sources of colour. Much medieval carving was treated using these naturally produced dyes. Later chemical dyes were developed to provide fade-free colours, and it was discovered that both oak and chestnut could be darkened by fuming with ammonia vapour.

Nowadays wood can be lightened, darkened or completely changed in colour with comparative ease, and the materials are readily available. Carvings can also be delicately tinted. The light colour of lime or sycamore, for example, can be given a warm and pleasant look by using an antique pine finish. More dramatic effects can be achieved by using stronger toned dyes.

The use of colour in either minor or major modes can certainly enhance a piece of work; equally, if used with total abandon it can have a disastrous effect. Some preliminary thought should always be given to the effect you wish to achieve, and wherever possible tests should first be made on scrap wood or off-cuts from the actual timber used. You may need to repeat part of the design on an off-cut, just to test out the colour effect, but time spent doing this is worth it. Never colour a carving without first testing.

Sometimes you may wish to colour only part of a carving: you might want to darken the background while leaving the design area in the original colour; or perhaps the other way around. In these cases, treat the parts you want to stay the natural colour with a heavy coating of wax (you do not need to buff it). This acts as a barrier, and prevents the dye penetrating these areas when you colour the rest of the carving.

STAIN OR DYE? Before looking in detail at some of the colour finishes you can use, it is worth clearing up a point which many people find confusing: what is the difference between a wood stain and a wood dye? In the old days, when life was simple, there never was any problem. Father stained the bedroom floor while mother dyed her hair. It was as simple as that, and everyone knew what you meant if you said you were going to stain a piece of wood.

These days, however, the term 'wood dye' is used to describe finishes suitable for use indoors, whereas 'woodstain' – now one word – relates to an exterior grade of treatment. This is a point to note should you ever need to colour a carving kept outdoors. In this section we shall be looking at some of the treatments suitable for carvings kept indoors. To simplify matters I have used the Liberon range of products as examples.

WATER-BASED DYES

These dyes are very traditional and some have been around for a very long time, such as Van Dyck crystals made from walnut husks, or bichromate of potash. More recently acrylic dyes have come to be generally used. They are available pre-mixed in a wide colour range and are very convenient to handle. Being water-based, the colour density can easily be changed.

Water-based dyes are easy to use, and are applied with a sponge or brush. They are slow to penetrate, so any surplus can be dabbed off with a piece of paper kitchen towel to vary colour density at will.

With some 'fluffy' woods, like lime, you will find the grain can rise as the dye dries, necessitating some sanding back. This can be reduced if the wood is wetted with cold water and allowed to dry before applying the dye, so any raised grain can be removed at that stage rather than after colouring. Be sure to sand gently with the lie of the grain.

SPIRIT DYES

Spirit-based dyes penetrate deeply. They may be preferable if the wood has a high natural oil content or a substantial resin content, as both these properties tend to repel the water-based varieties. If you are in any doubt as to which type of dye to use, test both on a piece of scrap wood.

Spirit dyes react quickly when applied to bare wood and their density can be difficult to control, especially when the end-grain is porous. This can lead to a blotchy finish.

In order to obtain a more uniform finish of end-grain, some pre-sealing of end-grain may be necessary. Use thin acrylic sealer or polyurethane matt varnish diluted by about 10 per cent with white spirit. Sometimes a weaker solution of the dye may be used to stain end-grain. It is best to use a pad of cloth and to apply the dye in small quantities, as application by brush is more difficult to control.

CONCENTRATED DYES

Concentrated dyes are available in both spirit and water-based forms, and can be added to standard dyes to alter or strengthen the colour.

TRANSLUCENT FINISHES

These finishes let the wood grain show through the colour. In some instances this can be an advantage, but translucent finishes seldom give you a complete colour change. As an alternative to proprietary makes you can use artists' waterproof inks.

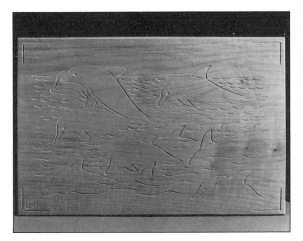

Fig 13.1 Incised carving after colouring cut lines. (Compare Fig 11.1)

OTHER COLOURING METHODS

You can colour wood with vegetable dyes, like the culinary types in little bottles, or try boiling up handfuls of leaves or roots. The results may not be very satisfactory, and rarely justify the time and effort involved. It is generally far better to buy reputable products designed for the purpose.

If you need only a very small amount of colour, use watered-down artists' acrylic paints. Experiment with colour density and dilution on a piece of scrap wood.

HOW MANY COLOURS DO YOU NEED?

There are two approaches to this question. Most dye manufacturers offer a wide range of pre-mixed colours (Liberon's 'Palette' series, for example, has 22 colours), which can be inter-mixed at will or added to with concentrated dyes to give a vast total range. Alternatively, you can work with the primary colours: red, blue and yellow. By mixing combinations of these, adding black or white to darken or lighten, an approximation of all other colours can be achieved.

WHEN AND HOW TO USE DYES

The degree of colour is very personal. A simple example would be when the undercut parts of relief carvings are darkened to increase the shadow contrast. Much old furniture carving was subjected to this treatment, but the choice of whether or not to use the technique is entirely up to you. Complex colouring can completely change the look of a carving.

Incised carving can be 'strengthened' if the cut lines are darkened: Fig 13.1 shows the dolphins from Chapter 11 treated in this way. Before carving, the wood was sealed with clear matt acrylic varnish, diluted by about 10 per cent to prevent the colour from bleeding over the surface. Three sealing coats were applied; each well sanded. After carving, all the incised lines were touched-in with artists' acrylic paint. You can see the difference between this picture and the untreated dolphins on page 108.

You may want only a subtle colour change to give a warm look to bland wood, as I mentioned earlier, or perhaps a dramatic poly-chromatic effect is needed. Refer back to the final photograph of the low relief carving in Chapter 8 (*see* page 83), which shows the untreated limewood. Now look at the example in the colour section. This is the same carving after it has been coloured with water dyes from the 'Palette' range.

To give the work luminosity, gold dust was sprinkled on and rubbed in once the dyes were dry. A spray fixative was then used, and the carving was finally sealed with matt acrylic.

GILT EFFECTS

It isn't difficult to obtain a gilded effect, and you don't have to go to the expense of using gold leaf. In all cases, though, gilding is more effective when the wood has been crisply carved.

First seal the wood with Fontenay base priming coat (available from Liberon, and from some antique restorers) and allow it to dry thoroughly. The base comes in different colours for different finishes: red for antique gold; yellow for bright gilt; black for silver or pewter effects.

For larger areas it is then best to use gilt cream, worked in with a short bristle brush and allowed to dry for 48 hours before buffing to a sheen. The gilt can be protected with a finishing liquid (also available from specialized manufacturers and antique restorers), which gives a light gloss. Small detail can be treated with gilt varnish applied with a fine artists' brush.

It is possible to produce an antique patination by using a darker shade of gilt cream in some areas, and using fine steel wool to cut back to the Fontenay base in others.

FUMING

This is an old practice using ammonia, which only works with woods containing tannic acid, such as oak and chestnut. It produces a warm colour, the degree of which depends on the length of time the wood is exposed to the ammonia vapour. Being the result of a chemical reaction, the look of fumed wood is quite different to the effect of using a dye.

All you need to fume wood is a reasonably airtight container to take the carving or furniture. You can make up a polythene tent, or use a garden cloche or dustbin. I even used the inside of a truck once for a very large table. You can use normal household ammonia cleaner, bought at a hardware store, and usually need only a shallow dish to hold the ammonia. If you are going to fume a large piece of work, or if there is a large volume of air in your container, you will need to double up on the number of dishes. Put the ammonia in the airtight container with the carving. After about two, or possibly three, hours of exposure to the ammonia vapour the wood will have turned to a mid-tone. The longer the wood is exposed to the ammonia fumes, the darker it will get.

After fuming, wash the wood with cold water and leave it to dry naturally before coating it with finishing oil and/or wax. Do take every precaution using ammonia. It can be harmful to your eyes, so wear goggles. (*See* also page 104).

Summary
▮ The most important thing is to experiment with colour.
▮ Use the same species of wood to make tests.
▮ If you want to colour only part of a carving, seal and wax the remainder before using a dye.
▮ Water dyes work slowly, and are very easy to use.
▮ Spirit dyes react fast, and soak into end-grain quickly. They can cause a blotchy look, so seal absorbent areas with diluted matt polyurethane.

SAFE WOODCARVING

When performed correctly, woodcarving is a relatively safe activity. But it is naturally wise to take a few simple precautions, especially when you are using power tools.

You should observe the following safety points **at all times.**

▌ **Always hold chisels and gouges correctly,** so that your fingers are **behind** the cutting edge of the blade. Never hold your tools or work with your hands in front of the blade.

▌ **Always cut away from yourself.** Never reverse a carving tool and cut towards your body, no matter how tempting this may seem. It is far safer to turn the wood round to a new position.

▌ **Keep your tools razor sharp.** Not only will they require less energy to drive them through the wood, but these is less chance of their skating over the surface. Blunt tools can easily slip and slide dangerously. What is more, if you are unlucky enough to cut yourself, the wound from a sharp blade heals quicker than that made by a blunt blade.

▌ **Don't work in a clutter.** Give yourself room to move, and only have a few tools out on the bench at any time.

▌ **Secure your carving wood** before you start to work.

▌ **Sweep up** after every session. It is uncomfortable to stand on wood chips for too long, and you may slip.

▌ **Throw away rags** used for applying oil or wax immediately after use. They can be highly combustible. Dirty wirewool can reputedly self-ignite, so don't keep old bits.

▌ **Adequate lighting and ventilation** are important – make sure your workplace has both.

▌ **Never carve when you are tired** or when your concentration is at a low ebb.

▌ **Safety glasses** approved for high impact should be worn, especially when working with power tools. If you normally wear spectacles buy a pair of ventilated safety goggles.

▌ **Use a dust mask** approved for hardwood fibres. Wood dust, even in small quantities, can irritate your eyes and nose. Prolonged exposure can have a lasting detrimental effect.

▌ **Wear approved ear muffs** when using power tools, as the noise can be harmful.

▌ **Get into the habit of using these safety aids** when band-sawing, routing, drilling, sanding or grinding, even if only for a few minutes.

▌ **Keep solvents in clearly-marked containers,** well out of reach of small children.

▌ **Lock up** your workshop when it is not in use.

▌ **Don't rush.** A good craftsmen never hurries.

▌ **An approved fire extinguisher** for use with electrical applices is a wise investment.

▌ **A first-aid kit is a must.**

CHAPTER FIFTEEN

TECHNICAL DRAWING

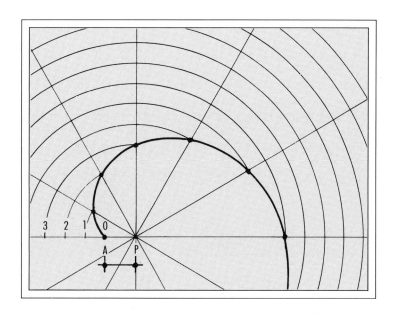

While much relief carving involves free-form drawing, there are times when it is necessary to use a more formal approach, often based on geometric principles. The following may be found useful in formulating designs.

For accuracy of working, good-quality drawing instruments are recommended. Use a screw-adjustable compass, or one which can be locked to a setting. For plotting directly on to wood, however, pointed dividers are usually more accurate.

BASIC CONSTRUCTIONS

TO BISECT A LINE: Fig 15.1

Line **AB**. Open the compass to more than half the length. With point on **A**, and then on **B**, strike an arc above and below the line. Then join the intersection above and below the line.

The line you have constructed divides **AB** into two equal parts and is at right angles to it.

TO BISECT AN ANGLE: Fig 15.2

Angle **XYZ**. Place compass point on **Y** and strike an arc to cut **XY** and then **ZY**.

With compass at same setting, place point at arc on **XY**. Strike an arc between the two arms of the angle.

Likewise strike a new arc from the point on **ZY**.

Where these new arcs intersect, draw a line to point **Y**. This line will bisect the angle.

TO CONSTRUCT A WELL-PROPORTIONED RECTANGLE – CREATING A GOLDEN SECTION: Fig 15.3

First draw a square. Bisect the bottom line to find the mid-point **A**.

Place your compass point on **A** and open the compass to the top right corner of the square **B**. Then scribe an arc to meet the extended base line **C**.

Complete the rectangle.

The rectangle can be divided into a square, and a rectangle, which is proportionally identical to the original rectangle. The new rectangle can be further subdivided in the same proportion to help fix points of design interest.

TO FORM A SQUARE AND RECTANGLE INSIDE THE GOLDEN SECTION: Fig 15.4

Set compass to short side of rectangle from point **A**. Swing arc to cut long side of rectangle at **B** and draw perpendicular to **C**.

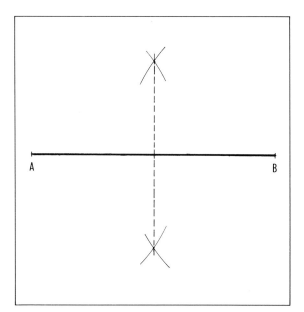

Fig 15.1 Bisecting a line.

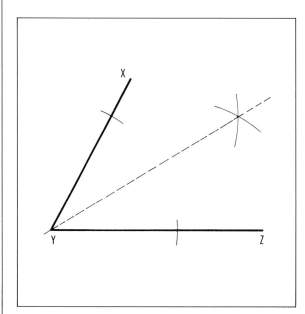

Fig 15.2 Bisecting an angle.

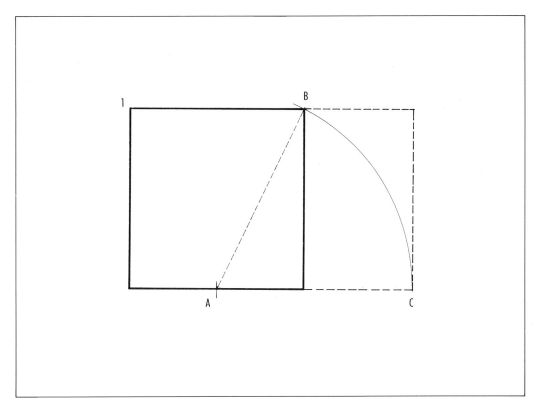

Fig 15.3 Creating a golden section.

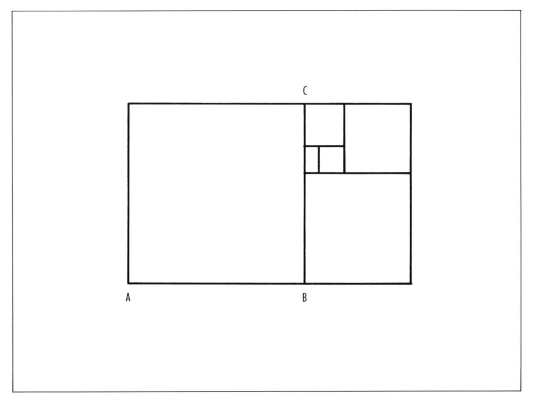

Fig 15.4 Sub-dividing a golden section into equally proportioned smaller squares and rectangles.

TO CONSTRUCT A REGULAR POLYGON HAVING EQUAL SIDES: Fig 15.5

A polygon is a shape with any number of sides greater than four.

First draw a circle approximately the size of the polygon you require.

Then draw the vertical diameter **B–C**.

Divide **B–C** into the same number of equal parts as there are sides of the polygon.

In the diagram the diameter has been divided into five equal parts by drawing line **B–D** from point **B** at an angle, and of a length, easily divided into five equal parts by measurement.

Point **D** is joined to **C5**. Other lines are then drawn parallel to it to divide the diameter at the other four points.

Then with compass point on **C** and opened to **B** strike an arc on the horizontal diameter extended out to **A**.

Strike a second arc with compass point on **B** to intersect the first arc at **A**.

Join point **A** to point **2** and extend to cut the circumference at **E**.

B–E is one side of the polygon. Step round the circle with compass set at **B–E** to complete the polygon.

TO DRAW AN ELLIPSE: Fig 15.6

The size of your panel may determine the length and width of the ellipse you require.

The length is called the major axis **e–f** and the width the minor axis **g–h**. Draw these two lines on your rectangle.

Make a trammel from a strip of card. Mark on it half the major axis and half the minor axis.

Place the trammel on the axis lines, so that the point marked for half major axis always touches the minor axis and the point marked for half minor axis always touches the major axis.

As you slide the trammel to sweep each quarter, mark points at the trammel end. After you have finished marking all the points, then join them up with a fair curve to form the ellipse.

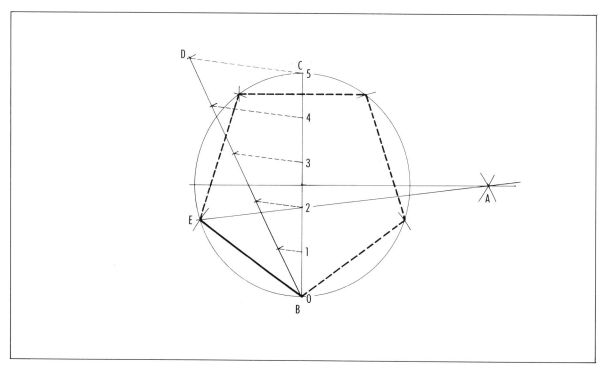

Fig 15.5 Drawing a regular polygon.

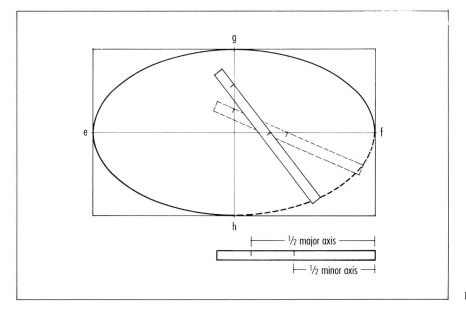

Fig 15.6 Drawing an ellipse.

TRACERY PANELS

Tracery panels often necessitate drawing circles inside other geometric shapes.

1. CIRCLES WITHIN SQUARES: Fig 15.7, 15.8 and 15.9

Diagonals are used to determine centres, Fig 15.7 and Fig 15.8. In the final square, Fig 15.9, angle **A** has been bisected to cut the centre line in order to find the centre of the first circle.

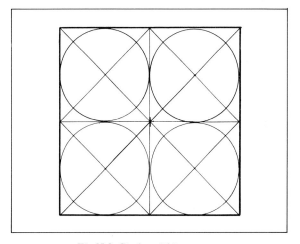

Fig 15.8 Circles within a square.

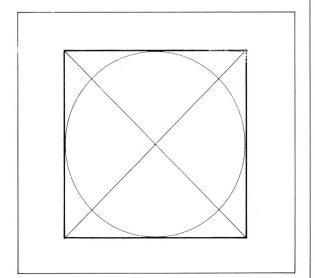

Fig 15.7 Drawing a circle within a square.

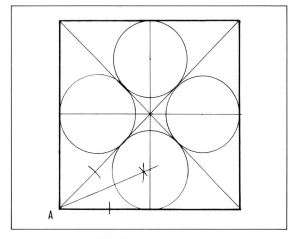

Fig 15.9 Circles within a square.

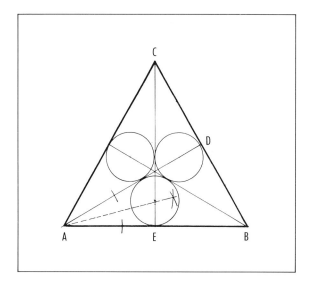

Fig 15.10 Drawing circles within a triangle.

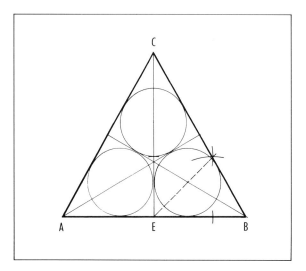

Fig 15.11 Circles within a triangle.

2. CIRCLES WITHIN TRIANGLES: Fig 15.10, 15.11 and 15.12

Start by using the construction shown in Fig 15.1 to bisect each side of the triangle. Angle **DAB** is bisected to intersect the line **EC** to find the centre for the first circle. Use this radius to form the other two circles.

In Fig 15.11, angle **CEB** is bisected to intersect the line drawn to bisect the angle of the triangle **ABC**.

Use distance **B** to the centre of the circle to find the centres of the remaining two circles.

This construction can be developed into the final trefoil type design (*see* Fig 15.12).

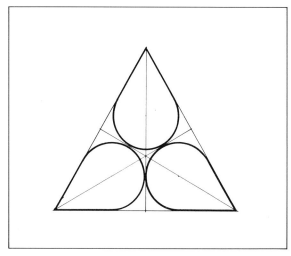

Fig 15.12 Extending the circles to form trefoil type design.

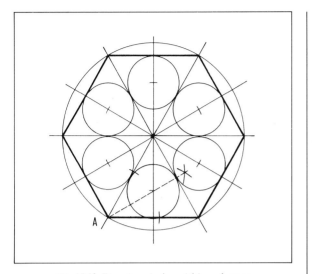

Fig 15.13 Drawing circles within polygons.

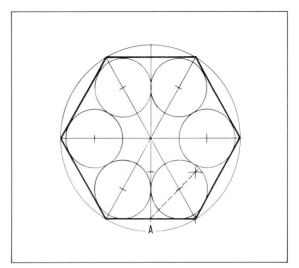

Fig 15.14 Circles within polygons.

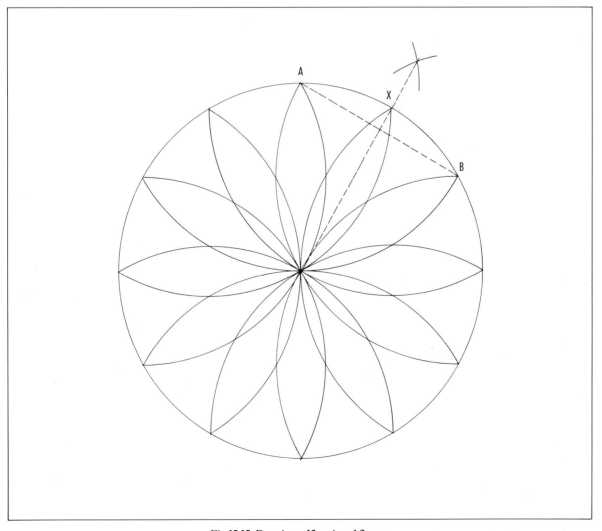

Fig 15.15 Drawing a 12-pointed flower.

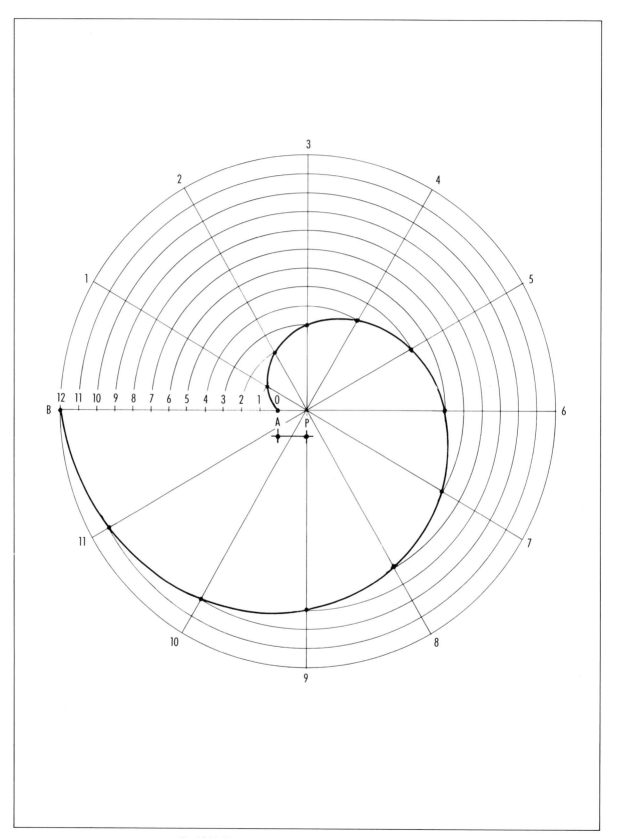

Fig 15.16 Drawing a scroll using an Archimedean spiral.

3. CIRCLES WITHIN POLYGONS: Fig 15.3 and 15.4

The polygon is divided into triangles and the previous construction can be used.

4. PETAL TRACERY: Fig 15.15

For petal tracery you need to set out a double hexagon (a 12-sided figure).

Fig 15.15. Keeping the compass set at the radius used to draw your basic circle, step round the circumference to find the first hexagon (6-sided figure).

Join one side of the hexagon **AB**. Bisect **AB** to find the mid-point, which will cut the circumference at a point on the second hexagon **X**.

Use the compass, set at the radius to step round the circle from **X**, marking the final 5 points of the second hexagon.

Place the compass point at each of the 12 points and scribe a semicircle, using the radius of the basic circle.

ARCHIMEDEAN SPIRAL

DRAWING A SCROLL USING AN ARCHIMEDEAN SPIRAL: Fig 15.16

Decide the starting and finishing points of your spiral. These are marked **A** and **B** on the circle centre **P**.

The section of the radius **AB** is divided into 12 equal parts.

The circle is divided into 12 equal segments (*see* Fig 15.15 for 12-sided figures).

Draw an arc joining point 1 on radius **BP** to radius **No 1**.

Take each point thereafter on radius **BP**, in sequence, and describe arcs to intersect their appropriate radii.

Draw a fair curve through the points to form tl Archimedean spiral.

IONIC VOLUTE

DRAWING AN IONIC VOLUTE: Fig 5.17

A scroll can be drawn using a whelk or similar spiral shell (*see* Fig 15.17). A large coach screw can also be used.

Tie cotton to the point of a pencil, then wind the cotton round the shell, following the spiral, so that the pencil point finishes close to the small, pointed end of the shell.

Unwind the cotton while holding the shell still – this permits the pencil to draw an Ionic volute.

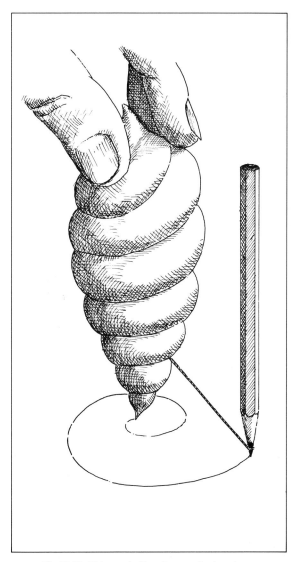

Fig 15.17 Using a shell to draw an Ionic volute.

INDEX

METRIC CONVERSION TABLE

INCHES TO MILLIMETRES AND CENTIMETRES						
MM = Millimetres CM = Centimetres						
INCHES	MM	CM	INCHES	CM	INCHES	CM
⅛	3	0.3	9	22.9	30	76.2
¼	6	0.6	10	25.4	31	78.7
⅜	10	1.0	11	27.9	32	81.3
½	13	1.3	12	30.5	33	83.8
⅝	16	1.6	13	33.0	34	86.4
¾	19	1.9	14	35.6	35	88.9
⅞	22	2.2	15	38.1	36	91.4
1	25	2.5	16	40.6	37	94.0
1¼	32	3.2	17	43.2	38	96.5
1½	38	3.8	18	45.7	39	99.1
1¾	44	4.4	19	48.3	40	101.6
2	51	5.1	20	50.8	41	104.1
2½	64	6.4	21	53.3	42	106.7
3	76	7.6	22	55.9	43	109.2
3½	89	8.9	23	58.4	44	111.8
4	102	10.2	24	61.0	45	114.3
4½	114	11.4	25	63.5	46	116.8
5	127	12.7	26	66.0	47	119.4
6	152	15.2	27	68.6	48	121.9
7	178	17.8	28	71.1	49	124.5
8	203	20.3	29	73.7	50	127.0

ABOUT THE AUTHOR

Jeremy Williams started carving at the age of fourteen, over forty years ago. His family's connection with woodcarving can be traced back to the early part of the 19th century. During the past fifteen years he has practised professionally with work sold widely both in England and overseas.

Jeremy is a fully qualified instructor with extensive teaching experience in Adult Education Centres, including Salisbury College of Technology.

Since 1982 he has run his own courses in woodcarving. These have proved to be popular with beginners, many of whom have been amazed with the results they have achieved.

More recently Jeremy has regularly contributed articles to *Woodcarving* magazine.

This is his second book. His first book, *Woodcarving Step-By-Step*, was published by The Crowood Press in 1992.

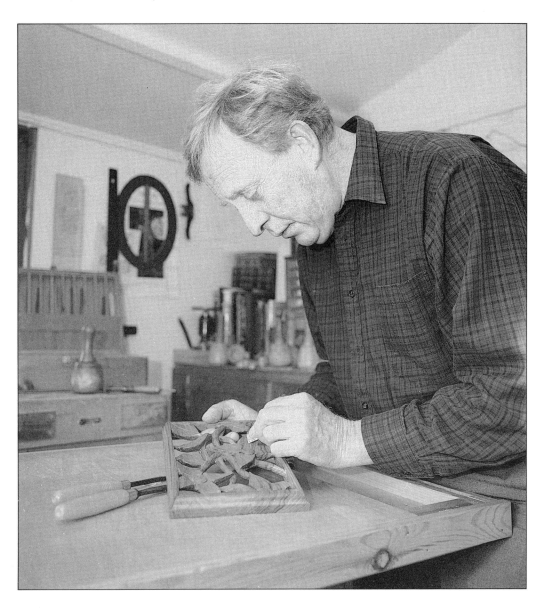

OTHER TITLES AVAILABLE FROM GMC PUBLICATIONS LTD

GMC Publications regularly produces new books on a wide range of woodworking and craft subjects, and an increasing number of specialist magazines, all available on subscription:

MAGAZINES

Woodturning   Woodcarving   Businessmatters

All these books and magazines are available through bookshops and newsagents, or may be ordered by post from the publishers at 166 High Street, Lewes, East Sussex BN7 1XU, telephone (0273) 477374.

Credit card orders are accepted. Please write or phone for the latest information.